International
Joint Ventures

International Joint Ventures

An Economic Analysis of
U.S.-Foreign Business Partnerships

Karen J. Hladik

Lexington Books
D.C. Heath and Company/Lexington, Massachusetts/Toronto

Library of Congress Cataloging in Publication Data

Hladik, Karen J.
    International joint ventures.

    Based on the author's thesis (Ph.D.—Harvard, 1984)
    Bibliography: p.
    Includes index.
    1. Joint ventures. 2. Investments, American. 3. International business enterprises.
I. Title.
HD2755.5.H58   1985   338.8′8973   84-40720
ISBN 0-669-09907-4 (alk. paper)

Published simultaneously in Canada
Printed in the United States of America on acid-free paper
International Standard Book Number: 0-669-09907-4
Library of Congress Catalog Card Number: 84-40720

Contents

Preface

The basic purpose of this book is to provide an up-to-date analysis of the characteristics of U.S.-foreign business partnership agreements. The main empirical studies of international joint venture activity date back to the early 1970s. Since that time, international joint ventures have become major competitive forces in many manufacturing industries including aerospace, pharmaceuticals, automobiles, and data-processing equipment, and it appears that there have been some significant changes in the characteristics of such partnership agreements. This book examines some of the dimensions of this change. It further analyzes the factors involved in certain key decisions in structuring the joint venture—decisions such as whether or not to undertake collaborative research and development (R&D) with a foreign partner or whether to export from the joint venture subsidiary or compete in the domestic market alone. Such decisions reflect both the joint venture's goals as a separate business entity and its role as part of a broader network of parent firm operations.

It is hoped that this book will provide one more step in our understanding of these issues and a potential source of ideas for future researchers in this field. Most of the book draws upon a new databank of information on 420 U.S.-foreign joint ventures formed between 1974 and 1982. The book is written primarily for the researcher interested in international business and international industrial organization. It might also, however, prove useful to the sophisticated practitioner who desires a more rigorous empirical overview of recent trends in international joint venture activity, particularly as they apply to U.S.-foreign R&D cooperation and export operations in manufacturing industries.

This book is based on research which I did at Harvard University and at the Harvard Business School. I would like to thank the Division of Research at the Graduate School of Business Administration, Harvard University, for their generous financial support through the Division of Research Fellowship Award program, which enabled me to devote almost all my time to this research and to compile the extensive dataset on which this study is based.

I also acknowledge with thanks the guidance and encouragement that I received from a number of professors, friends, and colleagues. I especially thank Richard E. Caves, of the Harvard Economics Department, who gave generously of his time and offered encouragement, direction, and many valuable suggestions throughout this research, and Michael E. Porter and M. Thérèse Flaherty, both of the Harvard Business School, who offered many suggestions and criticisms that were instrumental in sharpening the direction and content of this study. Louis T. Wells, Jr., also of the Harvard Business School, contributed several useful suggestions and ideas on the original research proposal and encouraged my interest in international joint venture activity. Finally, I thank Bruce Katz, Martha Cleary, and the editorial staff of Lexington Books. It has been a pleasure working with them, and I am sure that their experience and helpful advice have made this a better book.

1
Introduction

This book examines the changing characteristics of international joint venture activity between U.S. multinational firms and foreign partners in the manufacturing sector. This area of international business activity has received considerable attention since the late 1970s with well-publicized partnerships such as General Motors and Toyota in automobile production, AT&T and Philips in electronic equipment, and Pratt & Whitney and Rolls-Royce in aircraft engine development. Over this time, the number of U.S.-foreign partnership agreements has increased dramatically. One reason has been that multinationals have felt more resource-constrained in an increasingly competitive world economy. Another reason has been the growing protectionist sentiment against wholly owned operations in many host countries. As a result, a strategy of 100 percent ownership of worldwide operations has become unduly restrictive, if not impossible, for many U.S. multinational firms.

Given the importance of U.S.-foreign partnerships in many world markets today, it is unfortunate that so little information exists on this topic in recent business and economics literature. In part, this reflects the difficulty of obtaining the up-to-date data necessary to conduct any meaningful empirical analysis of this topic. Most recent information is, therefore, primarily anecdotal in nature.

This research has addressed some of these shortcomings in the literature by undertaking a large-scale database effort and compiling information on numerous characteristics of recent U.S.-foreign business partnerships. This effort has resulted in a databank of information on 420 U.S.-foreign joint venture partnerships formed between 1974 and 1982 in the manufacturing industries. The database has made it possible to identify and test various aspects of recent international joint venture activity including some of the factors involved in structuring joint venture pursuits such as collaborative R&D and export operations. As such, this book might prove useful to both the academic and the practitioner who desire a more rigorous empirical overview of the current nature of U.S.-foreign partnership agreements. Similarly, this book might be useful to the researcher who is constructing or working with a database on international business activity. The book provides considerable detail on the advantages and limitations of working with publicly available data and on the use of qualitative choice empirical techniques in business research. Given the virtual lack of empirical work on recent U.S.-foreign joint venture agreements, it is hoped that this research will begin to fill this gap and set the groundwork for further empirical analysis in this and other areas of international business activity.

The purposes of this book are (1) to acquire a better understanding of the changing characteristics of U.S.-foreign joint ventures since 1974 and (2) to examine rigorously the factors affecting the choice of some of these characteristics. Decisions involving two characteristics of recent international joint venture activity are singled out for separate treatment. The first involves the parent firm's decision of whether or not the joint venture will pursue its own R&D activities. The second involves the decision of whether the joint venture will export to foreign markets or compete only in the domestic market.

For the researcher who is new to this area, this book begins by reviewing some of the historical trends in international joint venture activity prior to 1975. This information is organized according to certain key characteristics—for example, the types of operations including manufacturing, sales, or R&D in which these earlier joint ventures were involved; export activities; ownership shares in the joint venture; location as between advanced and less-developed countries (LDCs); and characteristics of the foreign partners involved in the partnership. The lack of historical data and literature, unfortunately, limits the extent to which an exhaustive typology is possible. Nevertheless, enough information does exist on these key characteristics to establish a profile of earlier international joint venture agreements.

Against this background, this book presents new data on U.S.-foreign international joint ventures formed between 1974 and 1982. Using a newly compiled database on 420 U.S.-foreign joint ventures, it presents statistics on the number of international joint ventures formed each year, joint venture exports, joint venture R&D, U.S. ownership shares, and location of the joint venture. Much of these data are also cross tabulated by manufacturing Standard Industrial Classification (SIC) codes as a reference to the researcher who is interested in U.S.-foreign joint ventures in a particular industry sector.

This book uses this new database to analyze two characteristics of recent international joint venture activity in considerable detail. These are the joint venture's involvement in R&D operations and the joint venture's export activities. The theoretical framework that underlies the analysis is based on the existence of two sets of factors that can influence joint venture decision making: (1) the factors associated with the joint venture's own profit-maximizing opportunities as affected by its location, industry environment, and the resources at its disposal and (2) those factors associated with the activities of its parent firms and the interdependence of profits from these activities with the profits from the joint venture. This latter interdependence between joint venture and parent firm profitability can be negative, as in intersubsidiary competition in third country export markets. It can also be positive, as in know-how acquired through the joint venture being used to benefit other, parent firm operations. A model is developed to examine these various spillover effects and their impact on how parent firms might wish to structure joint venture activities.

In analyzing the R&D decision, probit maximum likelihood estimation techniques are used to test the effects of both joint venture and parent firm characteristics on the likelihood of joint venture involvement in R&D. The incidence of joint R&D is tested against factors such as market size, the technical know-how of one or both partners, and the minimum efficient scale of R&D in the joint venture industry. This book provides considerable depth of statistical analysis in support of the empirical findings and should be useful to the researcher interested in the use of qualitative choice empirical methods in economics or business research.

Similarly, this book considers both the joint venture's profit-maximizing opportunities and possible joint venture and parent firm interaction in analyzing the decision to export from international joint ventures. The factors tested include various country-, industry-, and firm-specific characteristics including the size of the host country market, economies of scale in production, and the international presence of both the U.S. and foreign partners. The empirical analysis is extended to consider the possible simultaneous determination of both joint venture R&D and export activity.

In conclusion, this study presents a summary of the various issues covered in this research including the major empirical findings. It is hoped that this study of international joint venture activity will both help and encourage future researchers in this area as many aspects of this complex yet important topic remain to be explored.

2

Historical Trends in International Joint Venture Activity: 1950–1975

Before examining the characteristics of recent international joint venture activity, this book begins by reviewing the state of our knowledge on international business partnerships and how it has evolved over the years. The historical data and literature, unfortunately, are far from complete. The seminal works in this area date back to Friedmann and Kalmanoff's[1] study of joint ventures in developing countries in the 1950s and the research done by Stopford and Wells[2] and Franko[3] on U.S.-foreign partnerships in the late 1960s. Since then, only a handful of studies has addressed this topic, mostly relying on case evidence to explore certain specific types of joint venture partnerships.

One of the difficulties that has hindered the study of international joint venture activity in the past has been the almost total lack of good statistical data on this subject. The Harvard Multinational Enterprise (MNE) Project,[4] on which the Stopford and Wells and Franko research is based, is one of the few available sources of statistical data on U.S.-foreign joint venture partnerships. It covers a sample of 180 U.S. multinational firms and includes information on several thousand foreign subsidiaries worldwide. The database, however, only extends through 1975. Thus, *traditional* joint ventures, as the term is used in this book, refer to joint ventures formed prior to 1975 and characterized by the various attributes discussed in this chapter.

Characteristics of International Joint Venture Activity: 1950–1975

The choice of characteristics of international joint venture activity largely reflects the topics on which earlier researchers have chosen to focus in prior literature. Particular attention, however, is also given to characteristics such as R&D and export activity that become important in later chapters.

Functional Activities

International joint ventures are not new to the foreign direct investment decision of the multinational firm. Prior to World War II, however, foreign

Table 2–1
**Joint Ventures by Principal Activity as a Percentage of Total Joint
Ventures Formed**

	Percent of Total Entries					
Activity	1951–1955	1956–1960	1961–1965	1966	1967	1968
Manufacturing	58%	72%	70%	70%	69%	72%
Sales and service	14	13	14	13	18	13
Extraction	11	3	2	1	4	4
Other	6	5	6	10	7	9
Unknown	11	6	8	6	3	2

Source: Calculated from data in Curhan, Davidson, and Suri (1977), table 6.1.1, p. 310.

Notes: A joint venture is defined as either a majority-owned (51–94 percent), co-owned (50 percent), or minority-owned (5–49 percent) foreign subsidiary of a U.S. parent firm. Data represent joint ventures newly entered into for that year. Joint ventures whose ownership shares are unknown (less than 5 percent of the total sample) are excluded from the sample.

Manufacturing applies to joint ventures that did any manufacturing, assembling, or packaging. *Sales and service* includes marketing, repair and maintenance, transport, storage, or finance. *Extraction* includes all raw material extraction, farming, and fishing. *Other* applies to joint ventures in holding, research and development, exploration, inactive, and other. See Curhan, Davidson, and Suri (1977), p. 6.

joint ventures were predominantly involved with trade, mining, or plantation agriculture. One of the most significant changes in international joint venture activity since then has been the increase in manufacturing joint venture subsidiaries.[5]

The importance of manufacturing joint ventures is confirmed in table 2–1. Between the early 1950s and 1975, manufacturing joint ventures accounted for 68 percent of total foreign joint venture activity by the U.S. multinationals in the Harvard MNE survey. Sales subsidiaries accounted for about 15 percent of foreign joint ventures during this time period, and extractive subsidiaries made up only about 4 percent (a sharp drop from over 10 percent in the early 1950s).

Other research—notably, Friedmann and Kalmanoff's study of joint ventures in less-developed countries (LDCs) in the 1950s—found that the parties were frequently "local manufacturers who have been operating in the field for some time, and the foreign investor who buys into the enterprise with the idea of expanding it."[6] Friedmann and Beguin note some 10 years later, however, that there had been a spread of joint venture activity from manufacturing into the exploration and production of minerals and other raw materials. Of this they write, "the most remarkable development is the introduction of joint venturing in the oil industry."[7] It is possible that this development accounts for the small percentage increase in extractive joint ventures in table 2–1 through the late 1960s.

| Percent of Total Entries | | | | | | | |
1969	1970	1971	1972	1973	1974	1975	Total Entries
65%	62%	67%	70%	70%	60%	66%	68%
14	16	15	17	16	22	18	15
6	4	6	3	1	6	5	4
10	14	9	10	11	12	9	8
5	4	4	1	0	1	1	5

Table 2–2 presents additional information on the relative importance of manufacturing joint venture activity. Aside from accounting for most of the joint venture subsidiaries being formed, manufacturing joint ventures also accounted for a large percentage of total (wholly owned and joint venture) manufacturing subsidiaries formed between 1951 and 1975. Joint ventures fluctuated between 29 and 48 percent of new manufacturing subsidiaries during that time. This was higher than in sales subsidiaries, where joint ventures accounted on average for only 16 percent of new subsidiary formation. Joint ventures were also predominant among extractive subsidiaries where they averaged around 35 percent of new subsidiary formation between 1951 and 1975.

Having noted the relative importance of manufacturing operations among international joint venture subsidiaries, one might ask if the scope of activity extends into other functional areas as well. One such area is R&D. The scarcity of information on this topic, however, seems to indicate that collaborative R&D was fairly uncommon in foreign joint venture subsidiaries in the 1950s and 1960s. Friedmann and Kalmanoff provide little evidence that R&D was being carried out in any of the joint ventures they studied in various developing countries, despite a clear desire by the host country governments to acquire technical know-how from U.S. parent firms.[8]

Similarly, neither Stopford and Wells nor Franko devote more than passing mention to collaborative R&D. In a survey sent to U.S. multinationals involved in joint ventures with foreign partners, the respondents ranked the importance of various types of contributions that the foreign partner could make to the joint venture. One category consisted of production, personnel, and R&D skills. This ranked fairly low: On an increasing scale of importance from 0 to 6, this category ranked 2.453 as compared to the lowest score of 2.451 and the highest score of 4.830.[9] While not conclusive, this result would be consistent with a low incidence of joint R&D in the sample.

Table 2–2
Joint Ventures by Principal Activity as a Percentage of Total Subsidiaries Formed

	Percent of Total Entries				
	1951–1955	*1956–1960*	*1961–1965*	*1966*	*1967*
Manufacturing Activity					
Wholly owned	64%	59%	52%	55%	60%
Joint venture	36	41	48	45	40
Majority owned	14	15	17	15	15
Minority owned	22	26	31	30	25
Sales					
Wholly owned	85%	85%	81%	81%	85%
Joint venture	15	15	19	19	15
Majority owned	6	5	7	3	6
Minority owned	9	10	12	16	9
Extraction					
Wholly owned	54%	74%	69%	77%	65%
Joint venture	46	26	31	23	35
Majority owned	25	12	11	8	12
Minority owned	21	14	20	15	23

Source: Calculated from data presented in Curhan, Davidson, and Suri (1977), table 6.1.1, p. 310.

Notes: In a wholly owned subsidiary, the U.S. parent has 95 to 100 percent ownership. In a joint venture subsidiary, the U.S. parent has 5 to 94 percent ownership. In a majority-owned joint venture subsidiary, the U.S. parent has 51 to 94 percent ownership. In a minority-owned joint venture subsidiary, the U.S. parent has 5 to 50 percent ownership. Joint ventures whose ownership shares are unknown are excluded from the sample.

It is possible, however, that the lack of R&D activity reflects, in part, the types of parent firms involved in joint venture activity. Stopford and Wells note that small firms rather than the industry leaders tended to favor joint ventures. Small firms were defined as those whose sales were less than one-half of the sales of the largest firm in the same primary industry. Stopford and Wells found that in 1966, 32.2 percent of the manufacturing subsidiaries of small multinational enterprises were joint ventures, compared to only 24.4 percent of the subsidiaries of large multinational firms.[10] Stopford and Wells also note the tendency of R&D-intensive firms to prefer wholly owned subsidiaries to joint ventures, another possible reason behind the low incidence of joint R&D in the sample.

Geographical Scope

The literature has characterized traditional joint venture activity as tending to be fairly localized in the country in which it is based. Stopford

			Percent of Total Entries					
1968	*1969*	*1970*	*1971*	*1972*	*1973*	*1974*	*1975*	*Total Entries*
71%	70%	66%	66%	67%	61%	60%	58%	61%
29	30	34	34	33	39	40	42	39
13	9	12	13	13	11	12	13	14
16	21	22	21	20	28	28	29	25
90%	88%	84%	88%	81%	82%	80%	76%	84%
10	12	16	12	19	18	20	24	16
4	3	6	4	8	9	3	3	5
6	9	10	8	11	9	17	21	11
70%	70%	52%	54%	55%	59%	68%	50%	65%
30	30	48	46	35	41	32	50	35
15	10	11	3	18	25	13	14	13
15	20	37	43	27	16	19	36	22

and Wells found that of the various benefits associated with having a foreign partner, general knowledge of the local economy, politics, and customs ranked highest on the list, followed by speed of entry into the local market (with mean ratings of 4.8 and 4 respectively on a scale from 0 to 6).[11] Factors that did not necessarily pertain to the local market and factors that would perhaps be most important to a global or regional joint venture ranked much lower. These included capital (2.7), access to local raw materials (2.6), and production, personnel, or R&D skills (2.5) as noted previously.

In Friedmann and Kalmanoff's research on LDC joint ventures, a discussion of the host country's foreign exchange considerations in evaluating joint venture prospects made no mention of the positive contribution of export sales.[12] The analysis focused primarily on the loss of foreign exchange associated with importing the production components from the foreign firm for sale in the host country.

Franko, writing 10 years after Friedmann and Kalmanoff, explicitly addresses the issue of export sales.[13] Joint venture exports, however, are found to be a problem for U.S. multinationals and a potential cause of joint venture instability. Franko's analysis of cases, articles, managers' comments, and questionnaires seems to indicate that intersubsidiary competition between the joint venture and other parent firm subsidiaries in export markets was a significant cause of joint venture instability. A questionnaire sent out to executives of multinational firms as part of the Stopford and Wells and Franko research appears to support this idea. In a ranking of ten problems typically encountered by executives of multinational corporations with their joint venture subsidiaries, markets to which the joint venture might export ranked second only to retention of earnings and dividends as a source of difficulty.[14]

Franko attempted to test empirically the hypothesis that conflicts over export market allocation were a cause of joint venture instability, using joint venture exit data generated as part of the Harvard MNE Project. The results, however, were inconclusive. Correlations between the importance of export market allocation problems and 1961–1967 joint venture instability rates were insignificant. Similarly, there was no evidence that a high degree of product tradability implied a high degree of joint venture instability.[15]

It appears, therefore, that despite the potential for conflict, the issue of joint venture export activity might have been resolved in many cases so as not to lead to the dissolution of the joint venture. There is some indication that this resolution tended to favor the foreign multinational parent. Stopford and Wells found that foreign parents were, in fact, often successful in exerting some degree of control over the sales of the joint venture to third country markets. The ways in which this could be done included (1) limiting the use of know-how and trade names to a specified geographical area and (2) transferring the responsibility for the joint venture's international sales to the foreign parent firm's marketing organization.[16]

The frequent use of such restrictions has been documented by other researchers.[17] These restrictions, particularly ones which gave the multinational parent absolute control over the joint venture's exports, often resulted in little or no export activity. There are indications that managers in multinational enterprises preferred to export from wholly owned subsidiaries rather than from joint ventures when given the choice.[18] While the foreign joint venture was useful in expanding the sales of the multinational's products in the host country market, exports were typically limited so they would not conflict with the multinational's other international operations.

U.S. Ownership Share

In both the LDCs and the advanced countries, there appeared to be a major shift from majority-owned to co-owned and minority-owned joint venture formation between the early 1950s and 1975. In LDCs, one of the important changes in international joint venture activity since World War II was the increasing involvement of local interests in these ventures.

Prior to that time, the principal partners were mainly foreign multinationals from advanced countries. If a local partner was involved, its role usually was very minor.[19]

By the end of the late 1950s, however, Friedmann and Kalmanoff characterized partnerships between developed countries and LDCs as being "an important phenomenon of the postwar period."[20] Many foreign multinationals, particularly U.S. firms, however, still preferred majority ownership. Nevertheless, Friedmann and Kalmanoff note that the incidence of minority ownership among foreign multinationals was much greater than is normally supposed. In about half of the cases they analyze, the foreign multinational held only a minority ownership share in the joint venture. Fifty/fifty partnerships, however, were found to be quite rare in private joint ventures though more common in special arrangements with the government. Friedmann and Beguin note a continuing trend toward multinationals' acceptance of minority participation in the 1960s.[21]

Table 2–3 supports the hypothesis that there has been an increasing trend in minority joint venture activity in LDCs. As a percentage of total subsidiary formation (wholly owned and joint venture), minority joint ventures appear to have increased substantially between 1951 and 1975, tripling from 8 percent of subsidiaries formed in the early 1950s to 23 percent in 1975. Majority joint ventures did not exhibit the same upward trend. Majority joint ventures rose only slightly from 11 percent of new subsidiaries formed in the early 1950s to 12 percent in 1975. Coownership, however, doubled over this time from 5 to 10 percent, also a significant change.

In the advanced countries, a similar breakdown of 10 percent involvement in majority joint ventures, 6 percent in 50/50 joint ventures, and 8 percent in minority joint ventures in the early 1950s resulted in a somewhat different trend from that in the LDCs. In the advanced countries, majority joint ventures decreased substantially to only 6 percent of the total subsidiaries that were formed in 1975, while minority joint ventures increased only slightly to 11 percent. Fifty/fifty joint ventures, however, nearly doubled, from 6 to 11 percent, becoming the most popular form of joint venture agreement (by a small margin over minority joint ventures) in advanced countries by the mid-1970s.

Geographic Location

Friedmann and Kalmanoff note that joint ventures have taken an increasingly prominent role in foreign investment activity in developing countries.[22] Between 1950 and 1957, the percentage of joint ventures to total U.S. foreign direct investment in LDCs increased from 11 to 17

Table 2–3
Joint Ventures by Location as a Percentage of Total Subsidiaries Formed

Ownership	Percent of Total Entries				
	1951–1955	*1956–1960*	*1961–1965*	*1966*	*1967*
Less-developed countries[a]					
Majority owned	11%	13%	13%	12%	15%
Co-owned	5	5	8	9	11
Minority owned	8	11	13	18	11
Total					
(5 to 94 percent)	24	29	34	39	37
Advanced countries[b]					
Majority owned	10%	8%	11%	10%	8%
Co-owned	6	9	10	9	6
Minority owned	8	7	9	8	8
Total					
(5 to 94 percent)	24	24	30	27	22

Source: Calculated from data presented in Curhan, Davidson, and Suri (1977), tables 2.1.4 (p. 22), 6.4.1 (pp. 362–363), 6.4.2 (pp. 364–365), 6.4.3 (pp. 366–367).
[a]Less-developed countries include Latin America, Africa, Mid-East (excluding Israel), South Asia, and East Asia (excluding Japan).
[b]Advanced countries include Canada, Europe, Israel, Japan, and South Dominions (Australia, New Zealand, and so on).

percent. In advanced countries, the percentage of joint ventures to total U.S. foreign direct investment rose from 22 to 31 percent, also a substantial though somewhat smaller rate of increase than in the LDCs.

Table 2–3 indicates that the divergence in joint venture growth rates between the LDCs and advanced countries continued through the mid-1970s. The increase in aggregate percentage joint venture activity was almost entirely fueled by the upward trend of joint ventures in LDCs. Joint ventures, as a percentage of total U.S. subsidiaries formed in LDCs, increased from 24 percent in the early 1950s to 45 percent in 1975. In advanced countries, this change was less significant: joint ventures increased from 24 percent of the subsidiaries formed in those countries in the early 1950s to only 28 percent in 1975.

One can conclude, therefore, that joint ventures have become an increasingly important form of foreign investment in LDCs, while their popularity has remained fairly constant in the advanced countries. Table 2–4 shows the percentage of joint ventures formed in LDCs and the percentage formed in advanced countries as a ratio of total joint ventures formed that year. Over the entire sample period, an average of 62 percent of the joint ventures were formed in advanced countries, and 38 percent were formed in LDCs. Since the early 1960s, the percentage of

			Percent of Total Entries					
1968	*1969*	*1970*	*1971*	*1972*	*1973*	*1974*	*1975*	*Total Entries*
15%	9%	12%	9%	15%	12%	8%	12%	12%
5	7	7	8	6	5	8	10	7
10	9	13	12	10	16	20	23	13
30	26	32	29	31	33	36	45	32
7%	6%	10%	8%	7%	9%	7%	6%	9%
6	7	8	8	10	10	8	11	9
4	8	8	7	9	9	9	11	8
17	21	26	23	26	28	24	28	26

joint ventures in the advanced countries to total joint ventures formed decreased to 51 percent of the sample by 1975. Correspondingly, the percentage of joint ventures in LDCs to total joint ventures formed increased to 49 percent of the sample in 1975.

Foreign Partners

U.S.-foreign partnerships can be classified into four categories:

1. A U.S. MNE and one or more local private firms;
2. A U.S. MNE and the local government, government agency, or state-owned enterprise (SOE);
3. A U.S. MNE and private local investors;
4. A U.S. MNE and a foreign MNE operating in a third country market with no local partner.

In their study of international joint ventures in the developing countries in the 1950s, Friedmann and Kalmanoff noted that "joint international business ventures in LDCs are generally between private companies from the capital-exporting country and private firms or small groups of investors from capital-receiving countries."[23] Cases of joint venture participation with large numbers of shareholders, however, were fairly limited. The study also found very little evidence of joint ventures with more than one foreign multinational partner (the study, however, does not consider joint ventures where there are no local partners as in category 4 of the list).

Table 2–4
Joint Ventures by Location as a Percentage of Total Joint Ventures Formed

| | *Percent of Total Entries* | | | | |
Location	1951–1955	1956–1960	1961–1965	1966	1967
Advanced countries	59%	58%	66%	61%	58%
Less-developed countries	41	42	34	39	42

Source: Calculated from data presented in Curhan, Davidson, and Suri (1977), Tables 2.1.4 (p. 22), 6.4.1 (pp. 362–363), 6.4.2 (pp. 364–365), 6.4.3 (pp. 366–367).

Conversely, Friedmann and Kalmanoff found joint ventures with the local government, government-controlled agencies, or SOEs to be fairly widespread in the LDCs they examined. They note, however, that U.S. firms tended to have a very different attitude than other foreign multinationals toward joint ventures with public concerns. Friedmann and Kalmanoff found that U.S. firms tended to view such arrangements with a great deal of suspicion. Unlike European firms, U.S. firms were "inclined to reject any such associations as inherently evil, as a token of socialism, and unacceptable to a free enterprise economy."[24]

During the 1960s, LDC governments not only encouraged more joint venture activity but also began to participate more actively as partners in major economic projects, especially projects involving public utilities or natural resources. The number and importance of joint ventures with governments in the LDCs thus increased substantially. More joint ventures were also formed between a greater number of partners. Friedmann and Beguin associate this trend from bipartite to multipartite joint venture activity with the increased capital needs of the larger-scale joint ventures being formed in the 1960s. These multipartite joint ventures often included companies of several nationalities, publicly distributed shares, the participation of the host government, or the involvement of national or international public lending agencies that provided capital resources for the project.[25]

Stopford and Wells focused on manufacturing joint ventures between a foreign multinational firm and local owners. The authors found that the local owners were usually "one or a small number of private partners holding large blocks of shares."[26] Fewer than 1 percent of the foreign manufacturing subsidiaries in the study were found to have publicly traded stock. Also, only sixteen joint ventures (less than 1 percent of the sample) were clearly identified as partnerships with the local government. This may, however, be an underestimation. The study notes

			Percent of Total Entries					
1968	*1969*	*1970*	*1971*	*1972*	*1973*	*1974*	*1975*	*Total Entries*
60%	68%	66%	65%	64%	62%	54%	51%	62%
40	32	34	35	36	38	46	49	38

that a lack of information may have caused some government joint ventures to be classified as unknown.[27] Furthermore, the sample excludes joint ventures in countries that require some degree of local ownership. If local participation in these countries often takes the form of partnerships with the local government or government agency, the study would also underestimate the percentage of such partnerships over a broader sample of countries. Tomlinson, for example, in a study of joint ventures in India and Pakistan (two countries not covered in Stopford and Wells's research) noted that multinational firms found host government associates to be very desirable as joint venture partners.[28] Finally, in the Stopford and Wells study, arrangements between foreign firms operating in a third, host, country were also found to be fairly rare and were excluded from the sample.

More recent data from the Harvard MNE Project show some interesting trends from the findings discussed earlier. Table 2–5 indicates how joint venture activity was divided among different types of outside owners in 1975. Joint ventures with local private owners were the predominant type of partnership agreement in manufacturing, sales, and extractive activity. What is interesting, however, is that joint ventures with other types of partners were fairly well represented as well. Joint ventures with local state partners accounted for 8 percent of the joint ventures formed for both manufacturing and sales subsidiaries and 23 percent among extractive subsidiaries. Widely dispersed equity holdings were even more popular in manufacturing and sales joint ventures, accounting for 11 and 9 percent of total joint venture activity respectively. Most striking, however, is the significant percentage of joint ventures between U.S. multinationals and other foreign (nonnational) private firms. Such partnerships were the second most popular type of agreement after joint ventures with local firms. They accounted for 14 percent of the joint venture subsidiaries formed in manufacturing, 28 percent of those in sales, and 31 percent of those in extractive activities.

Table 2–5
Joint Ventures by Principal Outside Owner as a Percentage of Total
Joint Ventures by Activity for Subsidiaries Active January 1, 1976

Owner and Ownership Share	Activity			
	Manufacturing	Sales	Extraction	Total
Local private				
Minority owned	22%	20%	16%	22%
Co-owned	24	21	8	23
Majority owned	16	11	15	16
Unknown	4	3	5	4
Total	67	55	44	64
Local state				
Minority owned	3	3	13	4
Co-owned	2	3	3	2
Majority owned	2	1	5	2
Unknown	1	1	2	1
Total	8	8	23	9
Foreign private				
Minority owned	7	13	16	9
Co-owned	4	10	7	5
Majority owned	2	4	3	2
Unknown	1	1	5	1
Total	14	28	31	17
Widely dispersed				
Majority owned	5	1	—	4
Co-owned	1	2	—	1
Majority owned	4	5	2	4
Unknown	1	1	—	1
Total	11	9	2	10

Source: Calculated from data presented in Curhan, Davidson, and Suri (1977), p. 374.
Notes: *Local private* refers to locally controlled private enterprises; *local state* refers to a local state agency or state enterprise; and *foreign private* refers to a foreign controlled private enterprise. If a subsidiary's stock is held by more than five independent partners and no one party holds a significant share of the equity, ownership is classified as *widely dispersed.*
  Ratios are calculated as a percentage of total joint ventures for which a principal outside owner has been identified. Unknown classifications are not included in the totals.

In addition, the type of partner chosen seems to be influenced by the size of the joint venture being formed. Table 2–6 shows, on the one hand, that as the size of the joint venture subsidiary increased to over $100 million, the percentage of joint ventures with local private firms decreased to only 44 percent of the joint ventures formed of this size. On

Table 2–6
Percentage of Joint Ventures by Size of Joint Venture Subsidiary
for Subsidiaries Active January 1, 1976

Owner and Ownership Share	Sales in 1975				
	Under $1 Million	$1–10 Million	$10–25 Million	$25–100 Million	Over $100 Million
Local private					
Minority owned	24%	24%	29%	17%	16%
Co-owned	29	25	23	18	10
Majority owned	21	19	14	16	10
Unknown	3	3	3	7	7
Total	77	71	68	57	44
Local state					
Minority owned	1	4	3	3	5
Co-owned	2	1	2	3	3
Majority owned	1	2	3	3	3
Unknown	—	—	—	1	3
Total	4	6	8	10	14
Foreign private					
Minority owned	7	5	6	10	16
Co-owned	3	5	5	4	5
Majority owned	2	1	3	1	4
Unknown	1	1	3	2	—
Total	13	12	16	17	25
Widely dispersed					
Minority owned	2	5	3	7	10
Co-owned	—	2	—	1	—
Majority owned	3	3	5	6	5
Unknown	1	1	1	3	2
Total	6	11	9	17	17

Source: Calculated from data presented in Curhan, Davidson, and Suri (1977), p. 382.

Notes: *Local private* refers to locally controlled private enterprises; *local state* refers to a local state agency or state enterprise; and *foreign private* refers to a foreign-controlled private enterprise. If a subsidiary's stock is held by more than five independent partners and no one party holds a significant share of the equity, ownership is classified as *widely dispersed.*

Ratios are calculated as a percentage of total joint ventures for which a principal outside owner has been identified. Unknown classifications are not included in the totals.

the other hand, partnerships with local state agencies, foreign private firms, and widely dispersed stock holdings became increasingly important in these larger size classes.

It would appear, therefore, that by the mid 1970s, U.S. MNEs were forming joint ventures with a somewhat more diverse set of partners than in the past. Joint ventures between U.S. MNEs and local private firms were still the predominant type of partnership arrangement, though agreements with government agencies, foreign private firms, and diverse groups of private investors were becoming increasingly important as well.

Summary

Chapter 2 investigated the characteristics of international joint venture activity by reviewing some of the prior research on this subject and how it has evolved over time. The impression one gets of traditional joint venture activity from this chapter is typically of a partnership between a foreign multinational and a private local firm that is limited to the manufacture of the foreign parent's products and fairly localized to the host country market. One of the questions that this book asks is whether this type of partnership has changed and why.

Notes

1. W.G. Friedmann and G. Kalmanoff, eds., *Joint International Business Ventures* (New York: Columbia University Press, 1961).

2. J.M. Stopford and L.T. Wells, Jr., *Managing the Multinational Enterprise* (New York: Basic Books, Inc., 1972).

3. L.G. Franko, *Joint Venture Survival in Multinational Corporations* (New York: Praeger Publishers, Inc., 1971).

4. The Harvard MNE Project is a large-scale, empirical study that was conducted under the auspices of the Division of Research, Graduate School of Business Administration, Harvard University. An overview of the data can be found in J.P. Curhan, W.H. Davidson, and R. Suri, *Tracing the Multinationals: A Sourcebook on US-Based Enterprises* (Cambridge, Mass.: Ballinger Publishing Co., 1977).

5. J.W.C. Tomlinson, *The Joint Venture Process in International Business: India and Pakistan* (Cambridge, Mass.: MIT Press, 1970), p. 5.

6. Friedmann and Kalmanoff, *Joint International Business Ventures*, p. 86.

7. W.G. Friedmann and J.-P. Beguin, *Joint International Business Ventures in Developing Countries* (New York: Columbia University Press, 1971), p. 19.

8. Friedmann and Kalmanoff, *Joint International Business Ventures*, pp. 129–130.

9. Stopford and Wells, *Managing the Multinational*, pp. 102–103.

10. Ibid., p. 139.

11. Ibid., p. 102.

12. Friedmann and Kalmanoff, *Joint International Business Ventures*, p. 202.

13. Franko, *Joint Venture Survival*, pp. 55–63.

14. Stopford and Wells, *Managing the Multinational*, pp. 103–104.

15. Franko, *Joint Venture Survival*, pp. 60–61.

16. Stopford and Wells, *Managing the Multinational*, p. 164.

17. See, for example, Friedmann and Beguin, *Joint International Business Ventures*, p. 370; Jose de la Torre, "Exports of Manufactured Goods from Foreign Developing Countries: Marketing Factors and the Role of Foreign Enterprise," Ph.D. dissertation, Harvard Business School, Cambridge, 1970; and Donald T. Brash, *American Investment in Australian Industry* (Cambridge: Harvard University Press, 1966).

18. Stopford and Wells, *Managing the Multinational*, p. 165. Similarly, Stopford and Wells find no examples of joint ventures whose assembly operations were primarily for export.

19. Tomlinson, *Joint Venture Process*, p. 5.

20. Friedmann and Kalmanoff, *Joint International Business Ventures*, p. 1.

21. Friedmann and Beguin, *Joint International Business Ventures*, p. 12.

22. Friedmann and Kalmanoff, *Joint International Business Ventures*, p. 21.

23. Ibid., p. 84.

24. Ibid., p. 272.

25. Friedmann and Beguin, *Joint International Business Ventures*, pp. 20–21.

26. Stopford and Wells, *Managing the Multinational*, p. 100.

27. Ibid., pp. 207–208.

28. Tomlinson, *Joint Venture Process*, pp. 137–138.

3
Joint Venture and Parent Firm Interaction

T his chapter broadens the analysis of international joint venture activity by providing the framework in which to examine the joint venture not only as a discrete unit in itself but also as part of the broader network of its parent firms' goals and objectives. This theoretical framework emphasizes the interaction between a joint venture and its parent firms' other operations in affecting the types of activities in which the joint venture becomes involved.

A Model of Joint Venture and Parent Firm Profitability

The economic literature has primarily concerned itself with analyzing the behavior of autonomous firms. Some recent literature, however, has addressed the types of relationships that can exist between two business units and how these relationships can affect market behavior. In particular, Flaherty discusses the interaction between two vertically integrated business units (not necessarily part of the same firm) and how this interaction can affect the coordination and product flow functions between the two units.[1] This book structures a simple model for dealing with the particular case of a joint venture whose behavior is not only affected by its own profit-maximizing objectives but also by those of one or both of its parent firms and the role that the joint venture plays in these firms' international strategies. The model concentrates on the interaction between the joint venture's activities and other, parent firm operations. These interaction effects are important in distinguishing the analysis of a joint venture from the analysis of an autonomous firm.

The following model considers the case of two potential joint venture partners, though the analysis can be extended to a coalition of three or more partners as well. The first party is assumed to be a profit-maximizing U.S. multinational firm that seeks to maximize the present and future expected profits of its total worldwide operations. The second party is a foreign entity, which we will label the *foreign firm*, that also maximizes present and future expected profits worldwide. Nonprofit objectives such as employment goals, foreign exchange generation, or technology transfer are treated as external constraints on the joint venture's activities and related to the particular host country environment in which the joint venture is based.

Each of the potential partners is endowed with a given set of tangible and intangible assets that it can choose to contribute to the joint venture.[2] Tangible assets refer to resources such as a firm's plant and equipment or its financial reserves that the market can value with relatively little ambiguity. Tangible assets can be specific to one country or can be noncountry specific. Furthermore, they can be specific to the particular firm, such as the local plant and equipment, distribution network, or labor force that the firm possesses.

The two partners may similarly pool certain intangible assets that can contribute to the joint venture's profitability. Intangible assets may take the form of country-specific resources such as experience and know-how in dealing with the local political and economic environment. They may also take the form of more general technical or managerial skills that can be applied profitably in more than one country.

The profitability of the joint venture is based in part on the complementary pooling of both tangible and intangible assets contributed by the two partners. Profits from the joint venture are then considered along with profits from the parent firm's non-joint-venture operations in determining the parent firm's total profit stream over all worldwide operations.

In order for the joint venture to exist, the following conditions must hold:

$$\pi = \pi_{NJV} + \alpha\pi_{JV} \geq \pi_A \tag{3.1}$$

$$\pi^* = \pi_{NJV}^* + (1-\alpha)\pi_{JV} \geq \pi_A^* \tag{3.2}$$

where

π = the U.S. MNE's discounted profit stream on total worldwide operations,

π_{NJV} = the U.S. MNE's discounted profit stream on all worldwide operations not including the joint venture,

π_{JV} = the total discounted profit stream on joint venture operations alone,

π_A = the U.S. MNE's discounted profit stream on total worldwide operations if the next most profitable alternative to the joint venture strategy is pursued,

α = the U.S. MNE's equity share in the joint venture,

π^* = the foreign firm's discounted profit stream on total world-wide operations,

π^*_{NJV} = the foreign firm's discounted profit stream on all worldwide operations not including the joint venture,

π^*_A = the foreign partner's discounted profit stream on total world-wide operations if the next most profitable alternative to the joint venture is pursued,

$(1 - \alpha)$ = the foreign partner's equity share in the joint venture.

These conditions state that for each partner, the sum of profits from non-joint-venture operations and its share of profits from joint venture operations must equal or exceed profits from the next most profitable alternative to the joint venture. Π_A and π^*_A may represent different alternative strategies. The next best alternative given the assets contractually attached to the firm, for example, might be to license intangibles to an independent firm, to export, or to establish wholly owned rather than jointly owned operations.

Host country laws and regulations may impose certain constraints. The value of α, the U.S. MNE's equity share in the joint venture, for example, may be constrained to be no greater than a certain percentage ownership share. Countries such as Mexico, Japan, or India, for example, have at various times set ceilings on foreign equity ownership in local enterprises. In this analysis, we assume that α and $(1 - \alpha)$ are determined outside of the system. Similarly, certain alternative strategies like wholly owned investment may not be feasible. Conditions (3.1) and (3.2) must therefore hold subject to the particular laws and regulations of the country in which the joint venture is based.

While the sum of joint venture and non-joint-venture profits must exceed profits from the next most profitable strategy, joint venture and non-joint-venture profits may be related. Either positive or negative interactions may exist. A positive interaction may exist, for example, when know-how that is gained from joint venture activities can be applied profitably to non-joint-venture operations as well. A negative interaction may result from competition between the joint venture and other parent firm operations, such as when geographical markets overlap.

Profit-Maximizing Conditions and Spillover Effects

This section discusses various conditions that can affect the profit-maximizing level of investment in joint venture activities. The analysis is presented from the perspective of one partner alone—here, the U.S. MNE. The next section considers a two-partner setting where different partners may have different profit-maximizing levels of activity.

We assume that the joint venture is formed and the decision between joint venture and alternative strategies has already been made. The level of investment in the joint venture is defined as I, where I is the sum of various different investment activities, based on the inputs of both partners into the joint venture: plant and equipment expenditures, the establishment of R&D facilities, export operations, and so on. I^* is then the value of I at which the U.S. MNE maximizes the sum of its joint venture and non-joint-venture profits.

I^*, however, may or may not be the same level of investment as that which maximizes profits for the joint venture alone. This level of investment depends on whether the joint venture and non-joint-venture profit functions are completely independent, whether negative spillovers exist between joint ventures and non-joint-venture operations, or whether positive spillovers exist. "Spillovers," as the term is used in this book, refer to the interactions between a parent firm's joint venture and non-joint-venture operations. The joint venture's activities can, therefore, have a neutral, negative, or positive effect on the profitability of non-joint-venture operations. These possibilities are discussed individually in the following sections.

No Interaction between Joint Venture and Non-Joint-Venture Operations

In the first case, the U.S. MNE's joint venture and non-joint-venture operations are completely independent. The joint venture's activities have no effect on the profitability of non-joint-venture operations. An example of the types of functional relationships that this could represent is diagrammed in figure 3–1. The joint venture's profit function and the U.S. MNE's total profit function are represented here as concave functions of I.

In figure 3–1 the profit-maximizing level of investment, I^*, in the joint venture occurs when

$$\frac{\partial \pi_{NJV}}{\partial I} = 0 \quad \text{and} \quad \frac{\partial \alpha \pi_{JV}}{\partial I} = 0$$

Where there is no interaction between joint venture and non-joint-venture operations, the U.S. MNE's profit-maximizing level of investment, I^*, is, therefore, identical to the level that maximizes profits for the joint venture alone. The joint venture is then treated as a profit-maximizing entity within the context of the U.S. MNE's worldwide network.

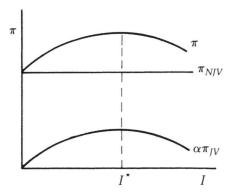

Figure 3–1. No Interaction between Joint Venture and Non-Joint-Venture Operations

The analysis of the joint venture should then be similar to that of an autonomous firm that is involved in that set of activities that maximizes its own profit function.

The literature has cited several examples of joint venture subsidiaries that have followed relatively autonomous strategies. In one study, a widely diversified, consumer-products company was described as allowing its joint venture partners to "do just about what they wanted as long as they paid adequate dividends and royalties."[3] This type of independence, however, was tolerated primarily among multinational parent companies that pursued highly decentralized strategies, allowing for a high degree of intercorporate diversity.

Negative Spillovers

In the second case, joint venture activities may negatively affect the profitability of the parent firm's non-joint-venture operations. Investment in a particular set of joint venture activities may reduce the profits of the parent firm's other operations. Since the parent firm's total profits are the sum of both joint venture and non-joint-venture profits, the gains to one may be offset by losses to the other. An example of this type of relationship is diagrammed in figure 3–2 for concave profit functions.

In figure 3–2, the profit-maximizing level of investment for the U.S. parent firm, I_{US}^*, occurs when:

$$\frac{\partial \pi_{NJV}}{\partial I} < 0 \quad \text{and} \quad \frac{\partial \alpha \pi_{JV}}{\partial I} > 0$$

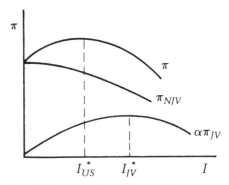

Figure 3–2. Negative Spillovers from Joint Venture Activity to Non-Joint-Venture Operations

where

$$\frac{\partial(\pi_{NJV} + \alpha\pi_{JV})}{\partial I} = \frac{\partial\pi_{NJV}}{\partial I} + \frac{\partial\alpha\pi_{JV}}{\partial I} = 0$$

In this case, the profit-maximizing level of investment, I_{US}^*, is less than the profit-maximizing point for the joint venture, I_{JV}^*, alone. The gains to investing further in the joint venture are offset by losses to other parts of the parent firm's corporate network. At I_{US}^*, the marginal profitability to the joint venture is equal to the marginal loss to non-joint-venture operations.

Several examples illustrate this type of situation. The joint venture's independently profitable expansion into foreign export markets, for example, may compete with the parent firm's existing operations in those countries. In the case of one firm in the chemical industry, it decided to sell out of its Italian joint venture "because we kept meeting ourselves all over Europe."[4]

The Asahi-Dow joint venture in petrochemicals is another example of how the expansion of the joint venture's operations may be constrained by the parent firm's profit considerations. In this case, Asahi-Dow joined Dow Chemical Co., its U.S. parent, in investigating lower cost raw material sourcing as an alternative to imports from Asahi Chemical, its Japanese parent. Disagreement arose over whether the joint venture was free to do so and hence free to increase its own profitability at the expense of its Japanese parent's profits on sales to the joint venture. The Japanese were against the move. One source was quoted as maintaining that "Asahi Chemical as the producer of ethylene, should worry about raw material problems for Asahi-Dow."[5]

Conflicts like these eventually contributed to the dissolution of the 50/50 Asahi-Dow joint venture in 1982. Both parents found that independent activity was more profitable than maintaining the joint venture.

In the chemical industry, one spokesman generalized just this type of parental constraint on joint venture activities in his industry:

> [M]any joint ventures in the chemical industry have two strong partners who have chosen to cooperate in the exploitation of a feedstock, a new process, or a new product. From an examination of such combinations, it is apparent that severe constraints were placed on the ventures, limiting their ability to grow and diversify their product line. In many cases, the joint venture must rely on one or more of the parents for technical support, which may or may not be forthcoming in a timely manner. Indeed, there is much evidence that more attention is given to narrowing the scope of the joint venture than in establishing a climate for independent activity.[6]

Positive Spillovers

In the third case, investment in joint venture operations also affects both the profitability of the joint venture's operations and the profitability of the parent firm's non-joint-venture operations. Here, however, the spillovers from the joint venture's operations actually favor expansion beyond the point of maximum profitability for the joint venture alone. At the extreme, the joint venture may even be unprofitable, though the benefits to non-joint-venture operations may be high enough to justify its existence. The types of functional relationships that this could represent are diagrammed in figure 3–3 for concave joint venture and total profit functions. In figure 3–3,

$$\frac{\partial \pi_{NJV}}{\partial I} > 0 \text{ and } \frac{\partial \alpha \pi_{JV}}{\partial I} < 0$$

where

$$\frac{\partial (\pi_{NJV} + \alpha \pi_{JV})}{\partial I} = \frac{\partial \pi_{NJV}}{\partial I} + \frac{\partial \alpha \pi_{JV}}{\partial I} = 0$$

Several examples illustrate positive externalities of this sort. In 1977, for example, the Coca-Cola Co. entered into joint venture operations where the stakes were considerably higher than the profitability of the joint venture. At that time, Coca-Cola formed a $10 million joint venture with the Egyptian government to develop a citrus plantation in

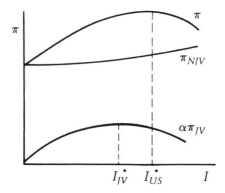

Figure 3–3. Positive Spillovers from Joint Venture Activity to Non-Joint-Venture Operations

the desert between Cairo and Ismali. This was done with the hope of ending the Egyptian boycott of Coca-Cola products that had been in force since 1967, when that company had awarded a Coca-Cola franchise in Israel. The strategy worked. A few weeks after Coca-Cola put down 25 percent of its $5 million share in the venture, Sadat lifted the boycott, allowing Coca-Cola the right to resume bottling in the highly lucrative Egyptian market.[7]

A strategic emphasis on global competition rather than on segmented, country-by-country battlegrounds has also resulted in some interesting examples of the interdependence of joint venture and parent firm profitability. IBM's recent joint venture with Matsushita to make small computers and office equipment, for example, seems to benefit IBM's operations more than the joint venture's own profit potential. By establishing a strong competitive presence in Japan, IBM has forced its Japanese competitors to redirect more of their resources to their home market.[8] The benefits of joint venture operation, in this case, extend to reduced competitive pressure on IBM's other subsidiaries and, hence, greater profitability for the parent firm as a whole.

Indeed, forefront research into the nature of global competition has found that multinationals may overinvest in one country or market in order to gain a competitive advantage in another. Hout, Porter, and Rudden cite the example of Caterpillar's construction equipment joint venture with Mitsubishi in Japan. Even though Caterpillar's Japanese operations earn only modest profits, they serve as an important check on the market share and cash flow of Caterpillar's much larger Japanese competitor, Komatsu, which competes with Caterpillar in markets throughout the world.[9]

Profit-Maximizing Conditions in a Two-Partner Setting

In a joint venture with a two-partner setting, each partner seeks to maximize its own total profit function that reflects the particular spillovers that it experiences between joint venture and non-joint-venture operations. Joint venture activity is thus affected by the profit-maximizing objectives of both partners and hence by the negative or positive spillovers that each partner might experience.

Issues in a Two-Partner Setting

The two partners may or may not differ in their assessment of the optimal level of investment, I^*, in the joint venture. Total investment in the joint venture is the sum of the U.S. MNE's investment and the foreign firm's investment. Given that the joint venture's profits are a well-behaved function of a vector of inputs, each partner will seek to contribute inputs into the joint venture up to its own marginal zero-profit condition for each input. These marginal optimization conditions yield a profit-maximizing set of inputs for the U.S. MNE and a profit-maximizing set of inputs for the foreign firm. The sum of these inputs can determine a total level of investment, I^*, in the joint venture at which both partners maximize total profits. Hence, there may be no problem with conflicting scale preferences, though I^* may still differ from the level of investment that maximizes profits for the joint venture alone.

The two partners, however, may disagree in their assessment of I^* under certain circumstances. One problem arises when the inputs of the two partners are complementary, such as when one partner contributes technical skills and the other contributes marketing channels. The two partners may desire different combinations of activities but have control over only part of the necessary set of inputs. Similarly, only certain combinations of inputs may be viable as in a Leontief-type production function where inputs must be combined in fixed proportions. The particular combination of inputs that is most profitable for one firm may differ from the profit-maximizing conditions for the other firm.

This section discusses some of the factors affecting the choice of investment in the joint venture when the profit-maximizing levels for the two partners differ. In other words, we assume the possibility of some total set of inputs (U.S. MNE inputs and foreign firm inputs) at which the U.S. MNE's total profit function is maximized. Similarly, we assume a potentially different set of inputs (U.S. MNE inputs and foreign firm inputs) at which the foreign firm's total profit function is maximized. The main purpose, however, is to show how, in a two-partner setting, the resulting level of investment in the joint venture may differ from the level that maximizes the joint venture's profits.

Two types of partnerships can be distinguished, depending on whether the foreign partner is or is not involved in non-joint-venture operations. In the first case, the joint venture is formed when the U.S. MNE buys an equity stake in an independent foreign firm. The partnership is then simply one between the foreign firm that retains part of the equity stake in its operations and the U.S. MNE that holds the remainder of the equity. In this case, π^*_{NJV} (the foreign firm's profits in non-joint-venture operations) $= 0$, and the conditions for the joint venture's existence are as follows:

$$\pi = \pi_{NJV} + \alpha\pi_{JV} \geq \pi_A$$
$$\pi^* = (1 - \alpha)\pi_{JV} \geq \pi^*_A$$

In the second case, both partners are part of broader corporate networks than the joint venture alone. Both are involved in non-joint-venture operations that may affect what they each perceive to be an optimal level of activity in the joint venture. Both partners can, therefore, find themselves in any one of the three situations discussed in the last section: independence between joint venture and non-joint-venture profit functions, negative spillovers, or positive spillovers.

U.S. MNE Equity Stake in an Independent Foreign Firm

In the first type of partnership, the U.S. MNE holds an equity stake in an independent foreign firm. Where the foreign firm is involved in no other operations beside the joint venture, it is clear that the profit-maximizing level of investment for the foreign firm is the same as the profit-maximizing point for the joint venture. For the U.S. MNE, the profit-maximizing level of investment may be greater, less than, or equal to the profit-maximizing point for the joint venture, depending on positive, negative, or zero spillovers between the joint venture and non-joint-venture operations. The case of negative spillovers is diagrammed in figure 3–4a.

We see that in figure 3–4a, the U.S. parent firm maximizes its total profits at the I^*_{US} level of investment in the joint venture. In figure 3–4b the foreign firm maximizes profits at I^*_F. Three factors determine the level to which the joint venture will expand its activities: (1) the profitability of alternative strategies for each of the partners, (2) host government regulations, and (3) bargaining dynamics including side payments and the role of uncertainty.

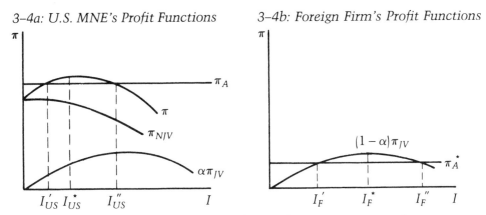

3–4a: U.S. MNE's Profit Functions   *3–4b: Foreign Firm's Profit Functions*

Figure 3–4. Profit-Minimizing Conditions for a U.S. MNE and an Independent Foreign Firm

In figures 3–4a and b, π_A is the next most profitable strategy for the U.S. parent, and π_A^* is the next most profitable strategy for the foreign firm. The U.S. parent will find the joint venture profitable only if it operates between I'_{US} and I''_{US}. The foreign firm only finds the joint venture profitable between I'_F and I''_F. A mutually profitable level of joint venture activity, however, can still be achieved between I'_F and I''_{US}, though this may not maximize either partner's total profit function.

Host government regulations are another factor that may set minimum or maximum limits on joint venture investment. In figures 3–4a and b, this factor may be embedded in the levels of π_A and π_A^*. The host government may place restrictions on certain alternative strategies such as wholly owned investment or exports into that country. This may lower π_A and make the U.S. MNE more amenable to a broader range of joint venture activity, I''_{US}. Similarly, host government restrictions may apply to certain specific components of the total level of investment, I, in the joint venture. The host government may stipulate that investment in the joint venture should include investment in export activities, the construction of large production facilities, the hiring of a substantial number of local workers, or R&D operations. These stipulations may result in some minimum level of investment that would set a lower bound on joint venture investment.

Finally, bargaining can also affect the level of investment on which the two partners decide. Under conditions of complete certainty, each partner would know of the profit functions and constraints facing the other firm. In that case, both firms would choose the level of investment, I^*, in the joint venture that would maximize the sum of the total profit functions for both firms. Side payments could then be negotiated such that the U.S. parent would receive π_A plus a fraction (α) of the residual profits generated above $\pi_A + \pi_A^*$. Similarly, the foreign firm would receive π_A^* plus its share $(1 - \alpha)$ of residual profits.

Under conditions of uncertainty, however, bargaining becomes much more complex. Each firm does better by convincing its partner that it faces highly profitable alternatives to the joint venture. The U.S firm would also want to overstate the negative spillovers that affect its non-joint-venture operations and understate any positive spillover effects.[10]

Two Partners with Non-Joint-Venture Operations

The preceding discussion considered some of the factors affecting joint venture investment when the U.S. MNE buys equity in an independent foreign firm. The analysis can be extended to the case where both partners are involved in non-joint-venture operations. Hence, it is possible to have three optimal levels of activity: (1) the level of activity that maximizes the total profits of the U.S. MNE, (2) the level of activity that maximizes total profits of the foreign firm, and (3) the level of activity that maximizes profits for the joint venture. It should be noted, however, that in the case where the foreign partner experiences no spillover effects between its joint venture and non-joint-venture operations, the situation is analogous to that described in the previous section. Here, we diagram the case where the U.S. MNE faces negative spillovers onto the profits of its non-joint-venture operations from joint venture activities and where the foreign firm faces positive spillovers (figure 3–5).

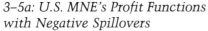 *3–5a: U.S. MNE's Profit Functions with Negative Spillovers*

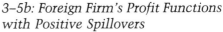 *3–5b: Foreign Firm's Profit Functions with Positive Spillovers*

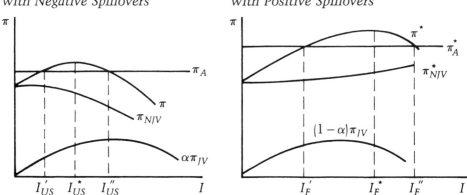

Figure 3–5. Profit-Maximizing Conditions for Two Partners with Non-Joint-Venture Operations

The same types of factors that were discussed earlier affect joint venture investments. Π_A and π_A^* represent alternative profitable strategies to the joint venture that place lower bounds on π and π^*. Host government regulations can affect the values of π_A and π_A^*. Π_A, for example, might have been higher had the host government allowed an alternative strategy such as wholly owned operations in its country. Constrained at its lower level represents less profitable, yet allowable, alternatives to the joint venture. Also, bargaining dynamics under conditions of uncertainty can affect the amount and type of investment in the joint venture. With both partners involved in non-joint-venture operations, however, the interrelationship of joint venture profits with profits from two different sets of parent firm operations adds to the complexity of the bargaining process.

To summarize, from this way of modeling joint venture agreements, one can see that the expansion of the joint venture's operations or, in the limiting case, its actual creation or dissolution can depend on several factors:

The profit function of the joint venture,

The impact of the joint venture's activities on the profit function of parent firm 1's non-joint-venture operations,

The impact of the joint venture's activities on the profit function of parent firm 2's non-joint-venture operations,

The profit constraints imposed by parent firm 1's next best profitable strategy after the joint venture,

The profit constraints imposed by parent firm 2's next best profitable strategy after the joint venture,

External constraints imposed by host country restrictions,

The bargaining dynamics between the two potential partners.

Applications to Joint Venture Characteristics

Up to now, we have been discussing total investment in the joint venture. Resources are invested in the joint venture that result in some level of profitability for the joint venture and possibly some positive or negative spillovers to the parent firms' other operations. This concept can be applied on a disaggregated level for decisions of whether or not to invest in specific types of investment activities. Decisions involving two particular characteristics of the joint venture are the decision to do R&D and the decision to export.

Total investment, I, as it has been considered up to now, is the sum of various types of investments in the joint venture. These investments can include investment in plant and equipment, the establishment of R&D facilities, export operations, distribution networks, and so on, represented as $I_1 \ldots I_N$:

$$I = I_1 + I_2 + I_3 \ldots + I_N$$

Consider the decision to pursue a particular type of investment, I_1. In the simple model that is discussed here, we assume that $I_2 \ldots I_N$ and α are fixed and that I_1 is the only decision variable under consideration. The model can also be formulated so that the profit-maximizing levels of $I_1 \ldots I_N$ are solved as a simultaneously determined system along with the equity shares, α and $(1 - \alpha)$, that the two partners hold in the joint venture, though this is considerably more complex. In both cases, however, the interaction between the joint venture and non-joint-venture operations of both parent firms is central to the investments that are pursued.

Joint Venture R&D

As one component of the total investment decision, the two partners may consider the establishment of R&D operations as part of the joint venture's activities. We assume a partial equilibrium analysis where all other components of investment, $I_2 \ldots I_N$, are fixed and I_1 (here, $I_{R\&D}$) is the only decision variable to be settled.

The analysis follows the general framework outlined in previous sections. Investment in R&D will depend on several factors:

The effect of joint R&D on joint venture profitability,

The effect of joint R&D on the profitability of the U.S. MNE's non-joint-venture operations,

The effect of joint R&D on the profitability of the foreign firm's non-joint-venture operations,

The lower bound on total profits for the U.S. MNE imposed by the U.S. MNE's next most profitable strategy after joint venture activity,

The lower bound on total profits for the foreign firm imposed by the foreign firm's next most profitable strategy after joint venture activity,

External constraints imposed by host country restrictions,

The bargaining dynamics between the two partners.

As presented in the previous section, the total profit function for each parent is the sum of both joint venture and non-joint-venture profits. Hence, the decision to undertake joint R&D must be evaluated both in terms of its effects on joint venture profitability and on the profits on non-joint-venture operations. Investment in joint R&D efforts may or may not affect non-joint-venture profitability. The three possibilities regarding possible interactive effects are (1) no interaction between joint venture R&D and non-joint-venture profits, (2) negative spillover effects, and (3) positive spillover effects.

In the first case, the decision to pursue joint R&D can be evaluated independently of the parent firm's non-joint-venture operations. It is possible, for example, that investment in R&D may, in fact, be profitable for the joint venture alone. As in the analysis of an autonomous firm, various country-, industry-, and firm-specific factors may be favorable for the joint venture's profitable pursuit of R&D operations. In the second and third cases, however, the role of the joint venture in its parent firm's operations must be considered as well. Negative externalities to the parent firm's non-joint-venture operations may make independently profitable joint R&D unprofitable for the parent firm as a whole. One can imagine situations where the parent firm is reluctant to share proprietary technical know-how with another firm, even a joint venture partner. In contrast, the parent firm might also experience positive externalities from joint R&D efforts. This can happen, for example, when experience and know-how gained from collaborative R&D efforts can be profitably applied to other parts of the parent firm's operations.

Host country regulations, however, may act as a constraint and require some minimum degree of joint R&D. In that case, a lower bound on allowable investment in R&D would exist. If such regulations cause total profits for either parent firm to fall below those of the next most profitable strategy, however, an alternative strategy may be pursued instead of the joint venture. Similarly, the final decision of whether to pursue R&D and to what level of activity may be influenced by the bargaining dynamics between the two firms.

The effects of several of these factors on joint R&D are testable. In particular, one can test whether the country-, industry-, and firm-specific variables that affect R&D in autonomous firms also affect joint R&D (that is, the importance of the joint venture's own profit function on the R&D decision). One can also test certain variables such as minimum efficient scale in R&D or the R&D intensity of the parent firm as indicators of interaction between joint venture and non-joint-venture operations (that is, the presence of negative or positive spillovers). These tests are pursued in chapter 5.

Joint Venture Export Operations

Another component of the total investment decision concerning the joint venture may be the decision to establish export operations. Again, it is assumed that all the other components of joint venture investment are fixed. The decision to export will depend on the same factors that affect an R&D decision:

The effect of joint venture exports on joint venture profitability,

The effect of joint venture exports on the profitability of the U.S. MNE's non-joint-venture operations,

The effect of joint venture exports on the profitability of the foreign firm's non-joint-venture operations,

The lower bound on total profits for the U.S. MNE imposed by the MNE's next most profitable strategy after joint venture activity,

The lower bound on total profits for the foreign firm imposed by the foreign firm's next most profitable strategy after joint venture activity,

External constraints imposed by host country restrictions,

The bargaining dynamics between the two partners.

The interaction between each parent firm's joint venture and non-joint-venture operations can also fall into one of the three categories: no interaction, negative spillovers, and positive spillovers.

Chapter 6 tests the effects of the joint venture's own profit function and the presence of spillovers between U.S. parent and joint venture operations on the joint venture's decision to export. In particular, it considers potential conflicts over third country markets. The joint venture's export into these foreign markets may interfere with a multinational parent's other operations in those countries. Chapter 6 considers specific interaction effects, depending on whether the joint venture and parent firm produce similar or dissimilar products.

Summary

Chapter 3 presents a theoretical model describing a joint venture's activities in the context of its parent firm's worldwide profit-maximizing objectives. The model concentrates on the interaction between a parent firm's joint venture and non-joint-venture operations. Depending on the positive or negative spillovers generated by the joint venture's activities as they affect the parent firm's other, non-joint-venture operations, parent firms may wish to over- or underinvest in the joint venture. The model is applied to decisions involving two particular characteristics of joint venture activity: the decision to do R&D and the decision to export.

The determinants of joint R&D and joint venture exports, including various interaction effects, are tested empirically in chapters 5 and 6.

Notes

1. M. Therese Flaherty, "Prices versus Quantities and Vertical Financial Integration," *Bell Journal of Economics*, Autumn 1981, pp. 507–525.

2. The concept of tangible and intangible assets is central to the transactional model of market behavior. See Oliver E. Williamson, *Markets and Hierarchies* (New York: The Free Press, 1983).

3. Lawrence G. Franko, *Joint Venture Survival in Multinational Corporations* (New York: Praeger Publishers, Inc., 1971), p. 32.

4. Ibid., p. 56.

5. "Asahi Chemical, Dow Chemical Dissolve their Joint Venture," *The Japan Economic Journal*, March 16, 1982, p. 16.

6. Arthur I. Mendolia, "The Life Cycle of Joint Ventures," *Chemistry and Industry*, December 1, 1979, p. 819. The author is chairman of CasChem, Inc., 40 Avenue A, Bayonne, N.J., 07002.

7. "Coke's Breakthrough into the Arab World," *Business Week*, April 10, 1978, p. 40.

8. "I.B.M. Aims Joint Ventures at Japan," *The New York Times*, March 21, 1983, p. D1.

9. Thomas Hout, Michael E. Porter, and Eileen Rudden, "How Global Companies Win Out," *Harvard Business Review*, September–October 1982, p. 98.

10. The game theoretic literature discusses the various types of bargaining strategies that firms can employ. In particular, see Howard Raiffa, *The Art and Science of Negotiation* (Cambridge: Harvard University Press, 1982).

4
Characteristics of International Joint Venture Activity: 1974–1982

C hapter 4 presents some new evidence on the characteristics of international joint venture activity between U.S. firms and foreign partners. This evidence is based on a new database compiled as part of this research and covers international joint ventures formed in the manufacturing sector between 1974 and 1982. The findings here seem to indicate a very different picture from traditional international joint venture activity prior to 1975.

Overview of Major Statistical Findings

Table 4–1 summarizes the findings on various characteristics of international joint venture activity between 1974 and 1982. The data pertain to joint ventures between a U.S. firm and a foreign partner based outside the United States. Each of the columns gives the number and percentage of joint ventures formed in that year by category. The data cover all manufacturing industries, as defined by the joint venture's primary SIC industry. By category, table 4–1 presents the following profile of international joint venture activity between 1974 and 1982.

Number of International Joint Ventures Formed per Year

The absolute number of international joint ventures appears to have increased significantly between 1974 and 1982. Except for 1974, the number has roughly doubled from the first 5 years to the latter 4 years of the sample period. The large number of international joint ventures formed in 1974, however, is a puzzle. 1974 could represent an outlier year in a general upward trend in international joint venture activity over time. Alternatively, it could indicate some degree of cyclicality in international joint venture formation. This latter hypothesis would also explain the small drop in the number of joint ventures being formed in 1981 and 1982.

Table 4–1
Characteristics of International Joint Venture Activity, 1974–1982

Characteristic	1974	1975	1976	1977	1978	1979	1980	1981	1982	Total
Number in sample	64	29	28	23	28	54	72	68	54	420
Number with exports	14 (22)[a]	10 (34)	7 (25)	8 (35)	6 (21)	20 (37)	38 (53)	35 (51)	24 (44)	162 (39)
Number with R&D	5 (8)	—	2 (7)	1 (4)	4 (14)	12 (22)	16 (22)	11 (16)	11 (20)	62 (15)
Number with nonmajority U.S. ownership[b]	32 (50)	18 (62)	13 (46)	16 (54)	15 (54)	29 (60)	43 (51)	34 (50)	30 (56)	230 (55)
Number with majority U.S. ownership[c]	7 (11)	3 (10)	5 (18)	2 (9)	5 (18)	8 (15)	9 (13)	13 (19)	9 (17)	61 (15)
Number with unknown percentage of U.S. ownership	25 (39)	8 (28)	10 (36)	5 (22)	8 (29)	17 (31)	20 (28)	21 (31)	15 (28)	129 (31)
Number in high-income countries	37 (58)	14 (48)	16 (57)	15 (65)	14 (50)	27 (50)	34 (47)	40 (59)	35 (65)	232 (55)
Number in mid-income countries	22 (34)	14 (48)	10 (36)	8 (35)	10 (36)	26 (48)	34 (47)	24 (35)	14 (26)	162 (39)
Number in low-income countries	2 (3)	1 (3)	—	—	2 (7)	—	4 (6)	2 (1)	3 (6)	14 (3)

Note: The countries are grouped according to World Bank classifications. Low-income countries include China, India, and other countries with a GNP per capita of less than $410 (1980 dollars). Middle-income countries include countries with a GNP per capita of between $420 and $4,500. High-income countries include the industrial market economies with GNP per capita of over $4,800. See *World Development Report 1982* (New York: Oxford University Press, 1982).

[a]Figures in parentheses are percentages of total joint ventures per year.
[b]Nonmajority is 10 to 50 percent ownership.
[c]Majority is 51 to 90 percent ownership.

Number of International Joint Ventures
with Export Operations

Export operations appear to be relatively common among the joint ventures in the sample. In the last 3 years of the sample, about half of the joint ventures formed each year were planning some amount of export activity. This represents an increase from the first part of the sample where only about one-quarter to one-third of new joint ventures were exporting. This activity is also in contrast with traditional joint ventures formed in the 1950s and 1960s that tended to serve only local markets.

Number of International Joint Ventures
with R&D Operations

R&D is not a particularly common characteristic among the joint ventures in the sample. Nevertheless, the percentage of joint ventures with R&D operations has increased over time from less than 10 percent of new joint ventures formed in the first 4 years of the sample to around 20 percent of new joint ventures in 1982. Even this percentage is surprising, however, given the rarity of U.S.-foreign collaborative R&D in the past.

Percentage Ownership by U.S. Parent Firm

Rows 4, 5, and 6 of table 4–1 indicate joint ventures that are minority or co-owned by the U.S. parent, joint ventures that are majority owned by the U.S. parent, and joint ventures for which the ownership shares are not known. The number of unknowns is problematic. U.S. minority or co-owned joint ventures, however, appear much more common than majority-owned joint venture subsidiaries. There is not much change in these relative ratios over time.

These findings on ownership share are roughly consistent with data from the Harvard MNE Project.[1] That research found that in both advanced countries and LDCs, the percentage of minority or co-owned U.S. joint ventures relative to majority-owned joint ventures had been increasing between the early 1950s and 1975. By 1975, about 79 percent of the joint venture subsidiaries formed in advanced countries and about 73 percent of the joint venture subsidiaries formed in LDCs were minority or co-owned. Of the joint ventures for which we have information in our sample, about 79 percent were minority or co-owned between 1974 and 1982.

Location of the Joint Venture

Rows 7, 8, and 9 of table 4–1 give the number of new joint ventures being formed in high-income, mid-income, and low-income countries respectively. The majority of the joint ventures in the sample were in high-income countries such as Japan, the United Kingdom, and France. Very few were located in low-income countries. There does not appear to be any clear upward or downward trend in any of these categories over the nine-year sample period.

Data from the Harvard MNE project, as presented in chapter 2, indicate a very similar split in the percentage of joint ventures in advanced countries and those in developing countries. In 1975, 51 percent of the joint ventures formed were in advanced countries and 49 percent in developing countries.

Database

Sources of Data

The purpose of creating this new database was to provide as comprehensive a list of recent U.S.-foreign partnerships as possible while still maintaining the depth of information necessary to examine specific characteristics of interest. Different mixtures of depth and breadth were possible. At one extreme, case studies of one or a small number of U.S.-foreign joint ventures provide a great deal of information on many of the specific details of joint venture activity. The difficulty, however, is in generalizing from so small a sample of observations to more aggregate trends in the nature of international joint venture activity.

At the other extreme, it is possible to work with some of the more aggregate listings of foreign subsidiaries and affiliates of U.S. firms. Disclosure data, for example, provide information on both foreign and domestic subsidiaries and affiliates of U.S. Disclosure parent firms in 1982.[2] After some sorting and adjusting of the data, one can derive a comprehensive listing of U.S. parent firms with foreign joint venture subsidiaries, the parent's SIC codes, and the percentage ownership, name, and location of the foreign joint venture. A small database of this sort was, in fact, developed at the early stages of this research.

The problems with the Disclosure data and similar types of aggregate listings was twofold. First, only the total stock of existing joint ventures was listed in a given year. Disclosure data only provided current information on the total stock of foreign subsidiaries and affiliates in 1982 versus a year-by-year flow of new joint venture subsidiary formation. Hence, it was impossible to investigate changes in international joint venture activity over time. Second, Disclosure and similar data sources supplied a minimal amount of information on the joint ventures. Aside from information on the U.S. firm's percentage ownership shares of the joint venture subsidiary and its location, it was difficult to know much more about what the joint venture actually did, who the foreign partner was, even the industry to which the joint venture belonged. Since the goal of this research was to investigate more fully the nature of recent international joint ventures, this was a serious shortcoming in available data of this sort.

The database that was eventually compiled falls somewhere in between the depth of case analysis and the breadth of foreign subsidiary listings like the Disclosure data. The principal source of information was the *F&S Index of Corporate Change*, a periodicals index published quarterly by Predicasts, Inc.[3] The *F&S Index* lists references to joint venture activity by U.S. multinational firms as they appear in its coverage of several hundred journals, magazines, and newspapers each year. It covers both foreign and domestic periodicals. In terms of the breadth of the database, it seems that most international joint venture activity would be captured in this literature.

Some limit on the time period and industrial scope, however, was necessary. 1974 proved a convenient starting point because this was the first year for which the *F&S Index* and many of the periodical sources were readily available to this researcher. The database was limited to joint ventures in the manufacturing industries, as specified by the SIC code classifications provided for each joint venture entry in the *F&S Index* (SIC codes 2000–3999). Joint ventures in industries such as mining and extraction, retailing, and banking were, therefore, excluded, partly out of manageability considerations and partly to maintain some degree of cross-industry homogeneity in the sample.

The depth to the database is based on the information provided in the periodical articles referenced for each joint venture. The amount of information, of course, varies from article to article. Nevertheless, the database does generally provide a great deal of information on the basic characteristics of joint venture activity such as the names of foreign partners, the range of activity undertaken by the joint venture, and the geographical markets covered by the joint venture. To my knowledge, this information is unavailable from any other existing database. Furthermore, in many cases, it includes interesting yet elusive bits of information such as motivations underlying the partnership, the individual partners' contributions, even stumbling blocks in the negotiations before the joint venture was finalized. Finally, the data provided here can be supplemented with information from additional sources. The database, therefore, provides a foundation on which to add further detail.

Methodology

The *F&S Index of Corporate Change* thus provided a convenient starting point from which to build the database. Nevertheless, many more joint ventures were referenced by the *F&S Index* than were included in our sample. In order to maintain the highest amount of consistency throughout the database, only those joint ventures that met the following criteria were included.

Joint Ventures Formed in Manufacturing Industries. Manufacturing industries were identified as those with SIC classification listings between 2000 (food and tobacco products) and 3999 (instruments and miscellaneous manufacturing). The *F&S Index* noted the SIC classification for each joint venture that it referenced.

Joint Ventures between a U.S. Firm and At Least One Foreign Partner Located Overseas. This criterion excluded partnerships such as joint ventures between two U.S. firms overseas, joint ventures where the U.S. parent was not a business firm, and joint ventures between a U.S. firm and a foreign partner based in the United States or Puerto Rico.

Joint Ventures that Are Finalized. An extensive "grey zone" was found to exist between preliminary negotiations and a finalized joint venture agreement. It is not clear where one would draw the line to separate data on actual joint ventures from strictly speculative reports. Clearly, very preliminary talks should not be included in the number of international joint ventures formed that year. Similarly, many joint ventures that were agreed to in principle were never finalized. In order to maintain the highest degree of objective accuracy and consistency, only those joint ventures that were finalized were included in the sample.

Joint Ventures in which the U.S. Partner Has 10 to 90 Percent Equity Ownership. The 10 percent minimum criterion was used to eliminate probable investment activity from true partnership agreements. Those joint ventures where the U.S. parent firm owned more than 90 percent of the equity were treated as de facto acquisitions and, therefore, also different in nature from our focus on partnership situations.

Joint Ventures that Are Newly Formed or Otherwise Newly Entered into by the U.S. Firm. This criterion eliminated a fair amount of data where the U.S. firm was selling equity in an existing overseas subsidiary to a foreign partner. Technically, the resulting partnership could still be classified as a joint venture if the U.S. multinational retained more than 10 percent of the equity. In most cases, however, such restructurings seemed more akin to a liquidation of foreign holdings by the U.S. firm than to the formation of a new entity. Combining the two types of data would destroy some of the homogeneity in the sample. Similarly, changes in equity shares between existing partners could not be characterized as representing a new joint venture that year.

Joint Ventures that Are Formed to Be Ongoing Partnerships. This criterion is used to distinguish partnership agreements from joint ventures that exist simply as part of an ongoing acquisition process. In many acquisitions, the acquiring firm buys equity in parcels rather than all at once. This database eliminates cases where an initial purchase of equity in a foreign firm (and hence potential joint venture activity, by definition) is subsequently followed by a purchase of the remainder of the equity (hence, acquisition and not joint venture activity). To eliminate these cases, the *F&S Index* was checked for 1 year following an equity purchase to see if further acquisition activity followed during this time.

Joint ventures that satisfied these criteria were then tabulated onto special data forms. The data were then screened to eliminate redundant citations. Redundancy could occur when two U.S. firms were involved in the same joint venture and the *F&S Index* listed their involvements separately under the separate company headings. Similarly, cross-year redundancies had to be eliminated. This could occur when information on the same joint venture appeared in two successive years in the *F&S Index*. The references had to be consolidated and reported only under the year in which the joint venture was formed.

Strengths of the Database

Several features of this database make it particularly attractive for the purposes of the research presented here and as a basis for future work in this area. To summarize and add to the earlier discussion on this point, the main advantages are as follows:

> The database provides breadth and completeness across manufacturing industries and across a significant span of time. It covers 420 international joint ventures formed in the SIC manufacturing industries between 1974 and 1982.

> The database provides an adequate amount of depth of information with which to investigate certain basic characteristics of international joint venture activity. These characteristics can then be compared to earlier literature as well as over the time period presented here to test for changes that might have occurred. The database conveniently starts in 1974, a one-year overlap with the last year of data collected by the Harvard MNE Project.

> The database provides frequent though unsystematic information on the reasons behind various partnership agreements. Information on the contributions of the various partners, quoted statements on the objectives of the joint venture, and references to the particular way in which the joint venture is expected to benefit the parent firms are crucial to our understanding of this topic.

> The database is a strong foundation on which to base future research on this topic, either by adding depth or breadth of information. It has purposely been designed to facilitate future research, and as such is not an end in itself.

Weaknesses of the Database

The weaknesses of the database are, unfortunately, closely intertwined with its strengths. The weaknesses stem from the biases inherent in working with information from publicly available sources, like those found through a periodicals listing. Two types of information gaps must be taken into account when using this database. The first has to do with joint ventures that are known to have been formulated in a given year (that is, they have been referenced in the *F&S Index*) but for which the referenced information is not available. Articles can be unavailable for a variety of reasons; for example, local libraries do not subscribe to the periodicals referenced, particular issues are missing, errors exist in the reference, or the reference is to a news release by a company that can be obtained only directly from the company involved. If information is available for 80 percent of the joint ventures referenced in a given year but not for 20 percent, one must consider whether that 20 percent is somehow different in nature from the rest of the sample and hence biases the sample by its omission. In this case, we assume that it does not. These assumptions are discussed in the next section.

A second type of information gap occurs when certain information is not included in articles that have been referenced. Ideally, each article would state all the information of interest on the tabulation sheets (export activity, R&D, percentage ownership shares, location, and so forth). This rarely happens, with omissions happening with greater frequency in some categories than in others. Information on the location of the joint venture, for example, is almost always available, while information on percentage ownership is often missing. The difficulty lies in determining whether one can infer anything from missing information on a particular characteristic. For some characteristics, it is possible that this means that the joint venture does not possess this attribute (R&D operations, for example). For other characteristics, however, the value of the missing observations is much more ambiguous.

This research takes into account the presence of these information gaps. It discusses the assumptions that are made to derive values for the missing observations for each of the various characteristics of international joint venture activity. The assumptions are then used to get a best guess approximation of true trends, leaning, where possible, to the conservative estimate of new trends.

Recent Characteristics of International Joint Ventures

Number of International Joint Ventures Formed per Year

The previous section discussed the various criteria necessary for a joint venture listed in the *F&S Index* to be included in our sample. To summarize, only the following joint ventures were included:

1. Joint ventures formed in manufacturing industries,
2. Joint ventures between a U.S. firm and at least one foreign partner located overseas,
3. Joint ventures that are finalized,
4. Joint ventures in which the U.S. partner has 10 to 90 percent equity ownership,
5. Joint ventures which are newly formed or otherwise newly entered into by the U.S. firm,
6. Joint ventures which are formed to be ongoing partnerships.

The *F&S Index* was screened for joint ventures that appeared to meet the requirements listed in the preceding section. In most cases, the short description given in the *F&S Index* was sufficient to distinguish the joint ventures that met the first, second, and sixth requirements. Information was then retrieved for the referenced sources and screened once again to see whether each joint venture met the third, fourth, and fifth requirements as well and thus belonged to the sample.

Unfortunately, not all the references were available. Hence, the sample was limited to only those joint ventures for which information was available and that met the six requirements listed based on this information and the information given in the *F&S Index*. Table 4–2 compares the number of joint ventures referenced in the *F&S Index* to the number in our sample. References could be unavailable for a variety of reasons, but we assume that the sample is not seriously biased by these omissions. Since some references were unavailable, it is also possible that missing joint ventures did not meet all the necessary criteria for inclusion anyway.

As was indicated earlier, the number of joint ventures formed per year appears to be increasing over time. An issue to consider, however, is the unusually large number of joint ventures formed in 1974. The question is whether the year is just an outlier in a general upward trend

Table 4–2
Data Availability on the Number of International Joint Ventures Formed per Year

Data	1974	1975	1976	1977	1978	1979	1980	1981	1982	Total
Total joint ventures referenced	80	34	32	32	45	85	100	112	79	599
Number of joint ventures in sample	64	29	28	23	28	54	72	68	54	420
Percent of total	80	85	88	72	62	64	72	61	68	70

in joint venture formation or whether it is an indicator of a certain amount of cyclicality over time. Figure 4–1 is a plot of these data. Though one would need additional data to address this question, it seems that one cannot rule out the possibility that cyclicality may be present. In particular, one would need a longer time series to treat this issue rigorously.

Table 4–3 shows how the number of joint ventures formed each year is divided among the 13 different manufacturing sectors. (Table 4–3 and other tables showing cross-industry data are located at the end of this chapter.) Over half of total joint venture activity is accounted for by three of these sectors: (1) chemicals and allied products, (2) machinery except electric, and (3) electric and electronic equipment. Other important sectors are metals and metal products and food and tobacco products. Wood products and furniture, textiles and apparel, and petroleum and energy products make up only about 3 percent of the sample.

Turning to the trends over time in each industry category, one finds that in most cases, the number of joint ventures formed per year does not conform to either a definite upward or downward trend. Electric and electronic equipment is perhaps the only category for which one sees a definite percentage increase in international joint venture activity over the sample period. In 1974, electric and electronic equipment accounted for just under 8 percent of total cross-industry joint venture activity. By 1982, the number of joint ventures in this sector increased to 22 percent of the total. The highly aggregate nature of the 13 manufacturing classifications, however, needs to be kept in mind. Each classification can include

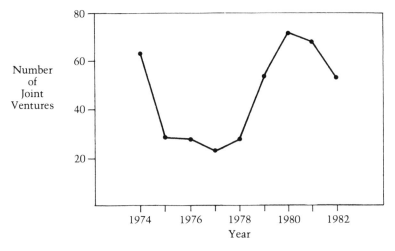

Figure 4–1. Number of International Joint Ventures Formed per Year

a diverse set of industries, resulting in only the most general trends for the manufacturing classification as a whole.

Number of International Joint Ventures with Export Operations

One of the characteristics in which this research is interested is the number of international joint venture partnerships involved in export operations. A joint venture was categorized as an exporter if the references indicated that the joint venture planned to pursue some amount of export activity. Typically, the information would indicate the markets in which the joint venture planned to compete. In certain cases, the specific export markets would be identified. In most cases, however, the joint venture would be described as planning to export or as exporting to various, unspecified, regional markets. Hence, the exact location of the export market would often be ambiguous.

The data were thus categorized into joint ventures with export activity and those for which there was no indication of export activity. An information problem, however, arose in this latter category. In some cases, the latter category included joint ventures that intended to compete only in the domestic market. In these cases, the joint venture could be unambiguously characterized as a nonexporter. In other cases, however, the information might indicate that the joint venture would compete in the domestic market but did not specify that this would be the only target of operations. In still other cases, this information would be missing. It is possible, therefore, that some of the joint ventures in these latter categories could be intending to export but that published sources had omitted this piece of information.

This research assumes, however, that the number of such misspecified joint ventures is quite small. It assumes that if, on the one hand, a joint venture is planning to export, this will be mentioned in published information on the joint venture's activities. If, on the other hand, the joint venture is not planning to export, sources may indicate that the joint venture will compete in the domestic market or leave this information out altogether as redundant. Hence, the mention of exports classifies the joint venture as an exporter, and mention of domestic markets or no mention of either domestic or international markets classifies the joint venture as a nonexporter.

Across different manufacturing industries, sectors with particularly high percentage ratios of export activity included electric and electronic equipment, instruments and miscellaneous manufacturing, and transport equipment (table 4–4). The ratio of exporting joint ventures to total joint ventures increased in most of the 13 manufacturing categories from the first half to the latter half of the sample period. This may be due to the highly aggregate nature of the industry categories, as we mentioned earlier.

Number of Joint Ventures with R&D Activity

Another major characteristic in which we are interested is the amount of collaborative R&D being done by U.S.-foreign joint ventures in recent years. Joint R&D was defined as any type of product or process development activity undertaken together by the two partners. Over the sample, this ranged from adaptive R&D, such as when a product or process was modified for a foreign market, to more basic types of innovative activity including cases where state-of-the-art products were being developed for global markets.

The information on each joint venture was screened to see whether or not it mentioned R&D activity. The information never specifically mentioned that R&D was not going to be pursued. An assumption, however, was made that if the published sources did not mention R&D activity, it was not done together by the two partners. It is possible that in a few cases, joint R&D was done but was not reported in the data. We assume that the number of these cases is small.

The results of the tabulation indicate relatively low levels of R&D in U.S.-foreign joint venture subsidiaries (table 4–5). The percentage of joint ventures with R&D operations, however, appears to be increasing over time. The percentage has almost tripled from the beginning to the latter years of the sample. An analysis of R&D across different manufacturing sectors is somewhat difficult because of the small number of data points available. Nevertheless, certain manufacturing categories appear to have a much higher percentage of R&D activity than others—notably, electric and electronic equipment, instruments and miscellaneous manufacturing, and textiles and apparel (though the small sample size in this latter category needs to be kept in mind).

Percentage Ownership of Joint Venture by U.S. Parent Firm

The U.S. parent firm's ownership share in the joint venture has been categorized as minority ownership, co-ownership, majority ownership, or unknown. Nonmajority ownership, as was presented in table 4–1, includes both minority-owned joint ventures in the sample (10–49 percent) and 50/50 partnerships.

Most of the data include some mention of the U.S. parent's equity share in the joint venture. When this information was missing, it posed certain problems. There is no reason to assume that missing data signify either minority, 50/50, or majority ownership. For the purposes of analyzing this characteristic, therefore, these missing observations were dropped from the sample, reducing the sample size available for empirical analysis. Table 4–6 reestimates the percentages of nonmajority and majority-owned joint ventures when the unknown observations are excluded from the sample.

It is striking to consider the large percentage of minority and 50/50 joint ventures that have been formed between 1974 and 1982 as estimated previously. An average of 80 percent of the new joint ventures formed over the sample were nonmajority joint ventures. There does not, however, appear to be much of an upward or downward trend over this time.

There also does not appear to be a broad discrepancy in ownership shares across different manufacturing industries as represented in tables 4–7 and 4–8. In most categories, 50 to 60 percent of the joint ventures were minority or co-owned by the U.S. parent. This figure is probably even higher if we drop unknown observations from the sample as was done for the aggregate figures.

Location of the Joint Venture

The final category to be considered here is the type of country, by income level, in which U.S. multinationals have formed joint ventures. Rows 7, 8, and 9 of table 4–1 give the numbers and percentages of joint ventures formed in low-income, mid-income, and high-income countries from 1974 to 1982. The residual between the number of joint ventures in the sample and the sum of rows 7, 8, and 9 consist of the small number of joint ventures whose classification fell outside the country groupings in table 4–1 (Eastern bloc countries, for example). Location information was available for all the joint ventures in the sample, and hence, we had no missing observations.

Certain countries were particularly popular as sites for U.S.-foreign joint venture activity. Among the mid-income countries, Mexico and Brazil accounted for a large percentage of the joint ventures formed in this country classification. Over the whole sample, however, Japan accounted for more joint ventures than any other single country. Table 4–9 shows the number of joint ventures located in Japan and the percentage of joint ventures in high-income countries that these numbers represent.

Tables 4–10 and 4–11 show the cross-industry distribution of joint ventures in high-income and mid-income countries. Of the larger industry groupings, industries in which joint ventures appear to be highly concentrated in high-income countries are instruments and miscellaneous manufacturing, electric and electronic equipment, and perhaps machinery ex electric. Joint ventures in transport equipment are concentrated in mid-income countries. Joint ventures in chemicals and allied products and metals and metal products appear to be evenly divided between high-income and mid-income countries.

Summary

Chapter 4 presents a profile of U.S.-foreign partnerships in the manufacturing sector between 1974 and 1982. It outlines some of the important characteristics of international joint venture activity during this time, including the number of joint ventures formed per year, exports, R&D, U.S. ownership share, and location. The results are based on a new database that was compiled as part of this research. This chapter describes the formation of this database, some of the advantages it has over alternative sources of data, and some of the difficulties compiling this type of database. It also discusses various ways in which the database can be extended for future research.

Table 4–3
Number of International Joint Ventures Formed in Manufacturing Industries per Year (Cross-Industry Data)

Manufacturing	1974	1975	1976	1977	1978	1979	1980	1981	1982	Total
Food and tobacco products (SIC 2000–2199)	9	4	1	4	2	3	9	9	3	44
Textiles and apparel (SIC 2200–2399)	1	—	—	1	—	2	3	2	—	9
Wood products and furniture (SIC 2400–2599)	—	—	—	—	—	—	1	—	—	1
Paper, allied products, printing (SIC 2600–2799)	3	1	3	—	1	4	—	—	2	14
Chemicals and allied products (SIC 2800–2899)	19	3	10	3	9	12	16	15	8	95
Petroleum and energy products (SIC 2900–2999)	—	—	—	—	1	—	1	—	2	4
Rubber, plastic, leather products (SIC 3000–3199)	1	2	1	1	1	—	1	4	1	12
Stone, clay, glass products (SIC 3200–3299)	3	2	3	—	1	5	2	1	4	21
Metals, metal products (SIC 3300–3499)	1	4	3	6	3	9	8	8	2	44
Machinery, except electric (SIC 3500–3599)	17	6	3	3	5	4	10	10	12	70
Electric and electronic equipment (SIC 3600–3699)	5	3	2	5	3	9	9	14	13	63
Transport equipment (SIC 3700–3799)	4	4	1	—	—	5	7	3	1	25
Instruments and miscellaneous manufacturing (SIC 3800–3999)	1	—	1	—	2	1	5	2	6	18
Total	64	29	28	23	28	54	72	68	54	420

Table 4–4
Number of International Joint Ventures in Manufacturing Industries with Export Activity (Cross-Industry Data)

Manufacturing	1974	1975	1976	1977	1978	1979	1980	1981	1982	Total
Food and tobacco products (SIC 2000–2199)	1 (11)	3 (75)	—	—	1 (50)	—	3 (33)	2 (22)	3 (100)	13 (30)
Textiles and apparel (SIC 2200–2399)	—	—	—	1 (100)	—	1 (50)	2 (67)	1 (50)	—	5 (56)
Wood products and furniture (SIC 2400–2599)	—	—	—	—	—	—	1 (100)	—	—	1 (100)
Paper, allied products, printing (SIC 2600–2799)	1 (33)	—	1 (33)	—	—	1 (25)	—	—	1 (50)	4 (29)
Chemicals and allied products (SIC 2800–2899)	3 (33)	—	2 (20)	—	1 (11)	5 (42)	8 (50)	8 (53)	2 (25)	29 (31)
Petroleum and energy products (SIC 2900–2999)	—	—	—	—	—	—	—	—	—	—
Rubber, plastic, leather products (SIC 3000–3199)	—	1 (50)	1 (100)	—	1 (100)	—	1 (100)	3 (75)	—	7 (58)
Stone, clay, glass products (SIC 3200–3299)	1 (33)	1 (50)	1 (33)	—	—	—	1 (50)	1 (100)	2 (50)	7 (33)
Metals, metal products (SIC 3300–3499)	—	1 (25)	—	3 (50)	—	3 (33)	5 (63)	5 (63)	1 (50)	18 (41)
Machinery, except electric (SIC 3500–3599)	4 (24)	2 (33)	1 (33)	2 (66)	—	2 (50)	5 (50)	4 (40)	4 (33)	24 (34)
Electric and electronic equipment (SIC 3600–3699)	3 (60)	1 (33)	1 (50)	2 (40)	2 (66)	4 (44)	4 (44)	7 (50)	8 (62)	32 (51)
Transport equipment (SIC 3700–3799)	1 (25)	1 (25)	—	—	—	3 (60)	4 (57)	2 (67)	—	11 (44)
Instruments and miscellaneous manufacturing (SIC 3800–3999)	—	—	—	—	1 (50)	1 (100)	4 (80)	2 (100)	3 (50)	11 (61)
Total	14 (22)	10 (34)	7 (25)	8 (35)	6 (21)	20 (37)	38 (53)	35 (51)	24 (42)	162 (39)

Note: Figures in parentheses represent the number of joint ventures with exports as a percentage of total joint ventures in that category per year.

Table 4–5
Number of International Joint Ventures in Manufacturing Industries with R&D (Cross-Industry Data)

Manufacturing	1974	1975	1976	1977	1978	1979	1980	1981	1982	Total
Food and tobacco products (SIC 2000–2199)	2 (22)	—	—	1 (25)	—	—	4 (44)	—	—	7 (16)
Textiles and apparel (SIC 2200–2399)	—	—	—	—	—	—	1 (33)	1 (50)	—	2 (22)
Wood products and furniture (SIC 2400–2599)	—	—	—	—	—	—	—	—	—	—
Paper, allied products, printing (SIC 2600–2799)	—	—	—	—	—	—	—	—	—	—
Chemicals and allied products (SIC 2800–2899)	1 (5)	—	1 (10)	—	—	3 (25)	3 (19)	1 (7)	2 (25)	11 (12)
Petroleum and energy products (SIC 2900–2999)	—	—	—	—	—	—	—	—	—	—
Rubber, plastic, leather products (SIC 3000–3199)	—	—	—	—	1 (100)	—	—	—	—	1 (8)
Stone, clay, glass products (SIC 3200–3299)	—	—	—	—	—	—	—	—	1 (25)	1 (5)
Metals, metal products (SIC 3300–3499)	—	—	—	—	—	2 (22)	1 (13)	1 (13)	—	4 (9)
Machinery, except electric (SIC 3500–3599)	1 (6)	—	1 (33)	—	—	2 (50)	3 (30)	2 (20)	2 (17)	11 (16)
Electric and electronic equipment (SIC 3600–3699)	—	—	—	—	3 (100)	4 (44)	1 (11)	4 (29)	4 (31)	16 (25)
Transport equipment (SIC 3700–3799)	1 (25)	—	—	—	—	—	1 (14)	1 (33)	—	3 (12)
Instruments and miscellaneous manufacturing (SIC 3800–3999)	—	—	—	—	—	1 (100)	2 (40)	1 (50)	2 (33)	6 (33)
Total	5 (3)	0	2 (7)	1 (4)	4 (14)	12 (22)	16 (22)	11 (16)	11 (20)	62 (15)

Note: Figures in parentheses represent the number of joint ventures with R&D as a percentage of total joint ventures in that category per year.

Table 4–6
Percentages of Nonmajority-Owned and Majority-Owned Joint Ventures in Reduced Sample, Excluding Unknowns

Ownership	1974	1975	1976	1977	1978	1979	1980	1981	1982	Total
Nonmajority-owned joint ventures	82%	86%	72%	89%	75%	78%	83%	72%	77%	79%
Majority-owned joint ventures	18	14	28	11	25	22	17	28	23	21

Table 4–7
Number of International Joint Ventures in Manufacturing Industries with Nonmajority U.S. Ownership (Cross-Industry Data)

Manufacturing	1974	1975	1976	1977	1978	1979	1980	1981	1982	Total
Food and tobacco products (SIC 2000–2199)	3 (33)	2 (50)	—	2 (50)	—	2 (67)	3 (33)	7 (78)	—	19 (43)
Textiles and apparel (SIC 2200–2399)	1 (100)	—	—	1 (100)	—	—	2 (67)	1 (50)	—	5 (56)
Wood products and furniture (SIC 2400–2599)	—	—	—	—	—	—	1 (100)	—	—	1 (100)
Paper, allied products, printing SIC 2600–2799)	2 (67)	1 (100)	1 (33)	—	—	2 (50)	—	—	1 (50)	7 (50)
Chemicals and allied products (SIC 2800–2899)	13 (68)	1 (33)	4 (40)	1 (33)	5 (56)	6 (50)	10 (63)	8 (53)	5 (70)	53 (57)
Petroleum and energy products (SIC 2900–2999)	—	—	—	—	—	—	1 (100)	—	—	1 (25)
Rubber, plastic, leather products (SIC 3000–3199)	1 (100)	1 (50)	1 (100)	1 (100)	1 (100)	—	1 (100)	1 (25)	—	7 (58)
Stone, clay, glass products (SIC 3200–3299)	1 (33)	1 (50)	1 (33)	—	—	4 (80)	2 (100)	—	4 (100)	13 (62)
Metals, metal products (SIC 3300–3499)	1 (100)	3 (70)	1 (33)	4 (67)	2 (67)	5 (56)	3 (38)	5 (63)	2 (100)	26 (59)
Machinery, except electric (SIC 3500–3599)	6 (35)	4 (67)	3 (100)	3 (100)	3 (60)	4 (100)	6 (60)	5 (50)	6 (50)	40 (57)
Electric and electronic equipment (SIC 3600–3699)	2 (40)	1 (33)	2 (100)	4 (80)	3 (100)	5 (56)	6 (67)	5 (36)	9 (69)	37 (59)
Transport equipment (SIC 3700–3799)	1 (25)	4 (100)	—	—	—	1 (20)	5 (71)	2 (67)	1 (100)	14 (56)
Instruments and miscellaneous manufacturing (SIC 3800–3999)	1 (100)	—	—	—	1 (50)	—	3 (60)	—	2 (33)	7 (39)
Total	32 (50)	18 (62)	13 (46)	16 (70)	15 (54)	29 (54)	43 (60)	34 (50)	30 (56)	230 (55)

Note: Figures in parentheses represent the number of nonmajority (10 to 50 percent ownership) joint ventures as a percentage of total joint ventures in that category per year.

Table 4–8
Number of International Joint Ventures in Manufacturing Industries with Majority U.S. Ownership (Cross-Industry Data)

Manufacturing	1974	1975	1976	1977	1978	1979	1980	1981	1982	Total
Food and tobacco products (SIC 2000–2199)	—	—	—	1 (25)	2 (100)	1 (33)	1 (11)	1 (11)	2 (67)	8 (18)
Textiles and apparel (SIC 2200–2399)	—	—	—	—	—	2 (100)	—	—	—	2 (22)
Wood products and furniture (SIC 2400–2599)	—	—	—	—	—	—	—	—	—	—
Paper, allied products, printing (SIC 2600–2799)	—	—	2 (67)	—	—	—	—	—	1 (50)	3 (21)
Chemicals and allied products (SIC 2800–2899)	1 (5)	—	3 (30)	—	1 (11)	2 (17)	4 (25)	3 (20)	1 (10)	15 (16)
Petroleum and energy products (SIC 2900–2999)	—	––	—	—	1 (100)	—	—	—	—	1 (25)
Rubber, plastic, leather products (SIC 3000–3199)	—	1 (50)	—	—	—	—	—	—	—	1 (8)
Stone, clay, glass products (SIC 3200–3299)	1 (33)	—	—	—	—	—	—	1 (100)	—	2 (10)
Metals, metal products (SIC 3300–3499)	—	—	—	1 (17)	—	1 (11)	2 (25)	1 (13)	—	5 (11)
Machinery, except electric (SIC 3500–3599)	2 (12)	2 (33)	—	—	1 (20)	—	—	3 (30)	2 (17)	10 (14)
Electric and electronic equipment (SIC 3600–3699)	1 (20)	—	—	—	—	—	2 (22)	3 (21)	2 (15)	8 (13)
Transport equipment (SIC 3700–3799)	2 (50)	—	—	—	—	2 (40)	—	—	—	4 (16)
Instruments and miscellaneous manufacturing (SIC 3800–3999)	—	—	—	—	—	—	—	1 (20)	1 (17)	2 (11)
Total	7 (11)	3 (10)	5 (18)	2 (9)	5 (18)	8 (15)	9 (13)	13 (19)	9 (17)	61 (15)

Note: Figures in parentheses represent the number of majority (51 to 90 percent ownership) joint ventures as a percentage of total joint ventures in that category per year.

Table 4–9
Number of International Joint Ventures in Japan

Location	1974	1975	1976	1977	1978	1979	1980	1981	1982	*Total*
Number in Japan	14	4	5	4	4	8	8	11	15	73
Number in high-income countries	37	14	16	15	14	27	34	40	35	232
Percent of high-income countries	38	29	31	27	29	30	24	28	43	31

Table 4–10
Number of International Joint Ventures in Manufacturing Industries in High-Income Countries (Cross-Industry Data)

Manufacturing	1974	1975	1976	1977	1978	1979	1980	1981	1982	Total
Food and tobacco products (SIC 2000–2199)	3 (33)	3 (75)	1 (100)	4 (100)	2 (100)	1 (33)	2 (22)	6 (67)	1 (33)	23 (52)
Textiles and apparel (SIC 2200–2399)	1 (100)	—	—	—	—	2 (100)	2 (67)	2 (100)	—	7 (78)
Wood products and furniture (SIC 2400–2599)	—	—	—	—	—	—	1 (100)	—	—	1 (100)
Paper, allied products, printing (SIC 2600–2799)	2 (67)	—	2 (67)	—	—	2 (50)	—	—	1 (50)	7 (50)
Chemicals and allied products (SIC 2800–2899)	10 (53)	2 (67)	5 (50)	1 (33)	4 (44)	5 (42)	7 (44)	5 (33)	5 (60)	44 (46)
Petroleum and energy products (SIC 2900–2999)	—	—	—	—	—	—	1 (100)	—	2 (100)	3 (75)
Rubber, plastic, leather products (SIC 3000–3199)	1 (100)	1 (50)	1 (100)	1 (100)	1 (100)	—	—	2 (50)	—	7 (58)
Stone, clay, glass products (SIC 3200–3299)	2 (67)	—	2 (67)	—	1 (100)	1 (20)	2 (100)	1 (100)	4 (100)	13 (62)
Metals, metal products (SIC 3300–3499)	—	—	1 (33)	4 (67)	1 (33)	5 (56)	3 (38)	6 (75)	1 (50)	21 (48)
Machinery, except electric (SIC 3500–3599)	12 (71)	4 (67)	2 (67)	2 (67)	3 (60)	3 (75)	6 (60)	4 (40)	6 (50)	42 (60)
Electric and electronic equipment (SIC 3600–3699)	3 (60)	2 (67)	1 (50)	3 (60)	1 (33)	6 (67)	4 (44)	11 (79)	11 (85)	42 (67)
Transport equipment (SIC 3700–3799)	2 (50)	2 (50)	—	—	—	1 (20)	3 (43)	1 (33)	—	9 (36)
Instruments and miscellaneous manufacturing (SIC 3800–3999)	1 (100)	—	1 (100)	—	1 (50)	1 (100)	3 (60)	2 (100)	4 (67)	13 (72)
Total	37 (58)	14 (48)	16 (57)	15 (65)	14 (50)	27 (50)	34 (47)	40 (59)	35 (65)	232 (55)

Note: Figures in parentheses represent the number of joint ventures in high-income countries as a percentage of total joint ventures in that category per year.

Table 4–11
Number of International Joint Ventures in Manufacturing Industries in Mid-Income Countries (Cross-Industry Data)

Manufacturing	1974	1975	1976	1977	1978	1979	1980	1981	1982	Total
Food and tobacco products (SIC 2000–2199)	5 (56)	1 (25)	—	—	—	2 (67)	5 (56)	3 (33)	2 (67)	18 (41)
Textiles and apparel (SIC 2200–2399)	—	—	—	1 (100)	—	—	1 (33)	—	—	2 (22)
Wood products and furniture (SIC 2400–2599)	—	—	—	—	—	—	—	—	—	—
Paper, allied products, printing (SIC 2600–2799)	—	1 (100)	1 (33)	—	1 (100)	2 (50)	—	—	1 (50)	6 (43)
Chemicals and allied products (SIC 2800–2899)	7 (37)	1 (33)	4 (40)	2 (67)	3 (33)	6 (50)	9 (56)	8 (53)	1 (13)	41 (43)
Petroleum and energy products (SIC 2900–2999)	—	—	—	—	—	—	—	—	—	—
Rubber, plastic, leather products (SIC 3000–3199)	—	1 (50)	—	—	—	—	1 (100)	2 (59)	—	4 (33)
Stone, clay, glass products (SIC 3200–3299)	1 (33)	1 (50)	1 (33)	—	—	4 (80)	—	—	—	7 (33)
Metals, metal products (SIC 3300–3499)	1 (100)	4 (100)	1 (33)	2 (33)	1 (33)	4 (44)	4 (50)	1 (13)	1 (50)	19 (43)
Machinery, except electric (SIC 3500–3599)	5 (29)	2 (33)	1 (33)	1 (33)	2 (40)	1 (25)	4 (40)	6 (60)	5 (42)	27 (39)
Electric and electronic equipment (SIC 3600–3699)	2 (40)	1 (33)	1 (50)	2 (40)	2 (67)	3 (33)	5 (56)	3 (21)	2 (15)	21 (33)
Transport equipment (SIC 3700–3799)	1 (25)	2 (50)	1 (100)	—	—	4 (80)	3 (43)	1 (33)	1 (100)	13 (52)
Instruments and miscellaneous manufacturing (SIC 3800–3999)	—	—	—	—	1 (50)	—	2 (40)	—	1 (17)	4 (22)
Total	22 (34)	14 (48)	10 (36)	8 (35)	10 (36)	26 (48)	34 (47)	24 (35)	14 (20)	162 (39)

Note: Figures in parentheses represent the number of joint ventures in mid-income countries as a percentage of total joint ventures in that category per year.

Notes

1. The Harvard MNE Project is discussed in chapter 2. For an overview of data on foreign joint venture subsidiaries of U.S. multinational firms, see Joan P. Curhan, William H. Davidson, and Rajan Suri, *Tracing the Multinationals: A Sourcebook on US-Based Enterprises* (Cambridge, Mass.: Ballinger Publishing Co., 1977).

2. Disclosure data include various financial and nonfinancial corporate statistics included in documents filed with the U.S. Securities and Exchange Commission. Disclosure data are available on the Harvard Program for Industry and Company Analysis (PICA) database for the current year only.

3. *F&S Index of Corporate Change*, Vols. 10–18 (Cleveland, Ohio: Predicasts, 1974–1982).

5
Determinants of R&D Activity by U.S.-Foreign Joint Ventures

T his chapter presents some empirical findings on the decision involving a particular characteristic of joint venture activity: the decision to do R&D. We assume that the choice of whether or not to form a joint venture has already been made, including the choice between joint venture and wholly owned operations. The chapter, therefore, focuses on the effects of various country-, industry-, and firm-specific variables on the likelihood of joint R&D and tests whether these effects have changed over time. It further addresses the question of why the percentage has increased so significantly in recent years. Table 5–1 shows how this percentage of U.S.-foreign joint ventures involved in collaborative R&D has changed over the 9 years covered by this study.

Whereas the literature on international joint venture activity is quite sparse, the literature on cooperative R&D between international joint venture partners is even sparser. Considering some of the potential benefits of joint R&D and the growing number of U.S. firms taking advantage of these opportunities, this research furthers our nascent understanding in this area.

Variables and Hypotheses

While the joint venture may be responsive to some of the same factors that make R&D profitable for autonomous firms, it may also be affected by the relationship between its activities and those of its parent firms. The economic literature provides some guidance as to the country-, industry-, and firm-specific variables that affect a firm's investment in R&D. We hypothesize that several of these factors affect joint venture agreements as well through the effect of R&D investment on the joint venture's own profit functions. In addition, however, the joint venture is affected by its role in the profit-maximizing objectives of its parent firms over all their operations. The interaction between the joint venture and its parent firms can also influence joint R&D.

Table 5–1
R&D Activity in U.S.-Foreign Joint Ventures

Joint Ventures	1974	1975	1976	1977	1978	1979	1980	1981	1982	Total
Number with R&D	5	0	2	1	4	12	16	11	11	62
Number in sample	64	29	28	23	28	54	72	68	54	420
Percent of total	8	0	7	4	14	22	22	16	20	15

The explanatory variables and their expected influence on joint venture R&D activity are as follows. A more detailed discussion of how the variables were compiled and the sources of data are given in the appendix.

Population (POP)

The *POP* variable stands for the population of the foreign country in which the joint venture is based. The profitability to the joint venture of undertaking R&D activity depends in part on the expected demand for the new product or process embodying the R&D. Schmookler, for example, has found market size and growth to be important stimulants to innovation.[1] His empirical work suggests that firms pursue innovative activity largely because of the economic rewards they hope to reap and that these expected rewards vary with the expected sales of the products embodying the invention.

As an influence on the joint venture's expected profits, the size of the host country market is, therefore, expected to be a positive factor affecting the joint venture's decision to pursue R&D. Population is used here as a proxy for market size and, hence, market demand. Market size, of course, reflects income per capita as well as population. The influence of income per capita, however, is factored out for separate treatment, as discussed later in this section.

International (INTL)

The *INTL* dummy variable is set equal to 1 if the joint venture intends to market its products outside the host country and 0 if otherwise. Market size depends not only on the size of the host country but also on foreign markets. Given the indivisible nature of innovation, the higher the revenues that the joint venture expects to draw from foreign markets; given its domestic sales, the higher its expected rate of return from R&D activities. Hence, there should be a greater economic incentive to pursue

R&D. Mansfield, Romeo, and Wagner, for example, have shown empirically that R&D investments are based on the revenues the firm expects to earn from both domestic and international markets.[2]

We should expect, therefore, that the joint venture's involvement in international markets should increase the expected return from proposed R&D activities. Therefore, *INTL* should be positively related to the likelihood that R&D operations are pursued in the first place.

Industry R&D (INDRD)

INDRD stands for average R&D expenditure as a percentage of net sales for all R&D-performing companies in the joint venture's industry in the United States. The positive influence of this variable on the joint venture's involvement in R&D should be twofold. First, high R&D/Sales ratios would, by definition, signify an industry environment conducive to R&D. The formation of a joint venture in a high R&D industry would most likely subject it to the same industry factors that make R&D profitable for other firms in the industry, controlling for the joint venture's technological opportunity set.

Second, aside from market conditions that can make it independently profitable for the joint venture to pursue R&D, high industry R&D ratios may also indicate a technically rivalrous competitive environment. A joint venture in such an industry might need to innovate to keep up with its competitors. Empirical evidence has suggested that competitors' R&D outlays may positively influence a firm's own R&D spending. Grabowski and Baxter, for example, tested a sample of eight chemical firms during 1947 to 1966 and found some support for a responsiveness among firms to each other's innovative activity.[3] For both of these reasons, a high R&D/Sales ratio in the joint venture's industry should be positively related to the joint venture's involvement in R&D operations.

Foreign Technology (FTECH)

The *FTECH* dummy variable is set equal to 1 if the foreign partner is judged to contribute technological know-how and resources to the joint venture and 0 if otherwise. The decision to pursue R&D may be influenced by the technological capabilities of one or both partners to the joint venture. If the foreign firm possesses important technical skills or resources and contributes them to the joint venture, we might expect the joint venture's R&D efforts to benefit. There should, therefore, be a positive relationship between this variable and the incidence of joint R&D in our sample.

Foreign Partner (FPARTNER)

The *FPARTNER* dummy variable is set equal to 1 if the foreign partner operates in international markets outside its home country and set equal to 0 if there is no indication of international scope. This variable attempts to capture whether the foreign partner is a multinational competitor in its industry. A strong partner, in this sense, may exert either a positive or a negative effect on the likelihood of joint R&D.

A strong partner will presumably facilitate the market penetration of the joint venture. Hence, as an indication of expected market demand, *FPARTNER* should positively influence the expected profits to joint R&D operations. Furthermore, where the foreign partner possesses important nontechnical assets (such as marketing skills or distribution channels), the U.S. MNE may need to transfer more technical know-how to make the joint venture attractive to the foreign firm. For this reason, a strong foreign partner might also be positively related to the incidence of joint R&D.

Conversely, some researchers have found that negative externalities may constrain a U.S. MNE's willingness to conduct joint R&D with a partner firm that is an important international competitor. One study, for example, found that several firms feared a strong competitor-partner's access to trade secrets transferred to the joint venture. In one case where the U.S. firm eventually bought out its British partner:

> It was the presence of the British competitor that had caused the lack of technological interchange, and now that the competitor-partner was gone, the American multinational could fully support the joint venture's R&D activities without risking the loss of proprietary information to a competitor.[4]

Similarly, the foreign partner may be reluctant to share its technological know-how with its U.S. partner. The foreign partner may also be less reliant on a joint venture partnership as a vehicle for doing R&D than would smaller, more localized foreign firms. For these reasons we might expect to see a negative relationship between *FPARTNER* and the incidence of joint R&D.

GDP per Capita (GDPC)

GDPC stands for the per capita GDP of the foreign country in which the joint venture is based. GDP data are expressed in $U.S. in constant 1980 prices. Population figures are based on annual International Monetary Fund (IMF) estimates for the year in which the joint venture is formed.

In addition to the foreign partner's technical contributions, one might expect that the general technical environment of the host country should affect the decision to establish joint R&D operations. A higher GDP per capita in the host country might indicate a greater abundance of scientists and technicians as well as better technical, informational, and communications facilities. We should, therefore, expect to see *GDPC* positively related to the likelihood of a joint venture based in that country pursuing R&D activity.

GDPC may also indicate a component of market size. We have already hypothesized a positive relationship between the size of the host country market and joint venture R&D. Hence, there is further reason to believe that *GDPC* will positively affect the likelihood of joint R&D activity.

U.S. R&D/Sales (USRDS)

USRDS is the R&D expense as a percentage of net sales for the U.S. parent firm. The R&D intensity of the U.S. parent firm may exert either a positive or a negative effect on the likelihood of joint R&D operations. The effect depends on the willingness of the U.S. parent to contribute its technical know-how and resources.

USRDS may have a symmetrical effect to that of *FTECH*. If the U.S. partner possesses important technical skills or resources and contributes them to the joint venture, R&D may be a more profitable undertaking for the joint venture than if it had no access to this know-how. The U.S. firm's R&D intensity should then positively affect the likelihood of joint R&D.

In contrast, an R&D-intensive parent firm may choose not to transfer its know-how to the joint venture and act to discourage joint R&D. In this way, *USRDS* can differ from the effect of *FTECH*. *FTECH* only controls for product or process technology that the foreign firm contributes to the joint venture. A U.S. parent firm that pursues a highly innovative strategy in its industry can be both highly efficient in its R&D efforts and protective about the technical know-how that gives it its competitive edge. As an efficient producer of innovative output, the parent firm might find it more profitable to conduct R&D itself and license the R&D to the joint venture. As a possessor of proprietary technical know-how, the parent firm might fear the leakage of technical secrets if transferred outside its wholly owned network. A negative relationship might, therefore, exist between the U.S. firm's technical superiority and the pursuit of R&D efforts by its joint venture subsidiary.

Table 5–2
Expected Effect of Variables on the Incidence of R&D Activity in U.S.-Foreign Joint Venture Subsidiaries

Variable	Expected Sign
POP	+
INTL	+
INDRD	+
FTECH	+
FPARTNER	+ or −
GDPC	+
USRDS	+ or −
MES	−
GOVT	+

Minimum Efficient Scale (MES)

The *MES* variable is the minimum efficient scale of R&D in the joint venture's industry. In many industries, there may be substantial scale economies to the profitable pursuit of R&D activities. A high minimum efficient scale of R&D might argue against decentralization of R&D effort away from the U.S. parent firm's main R&D facilities. Assuming a minimum efficient scale of R&D beyond that warranted by the joint venture's domestic and international markets, we might see a negative effect of this variable on the likelihood of joint R&D activities.

Government Involvement (GOVT)

The *GOVT* dummy variable is set equal to 1 if the host country government actively promotes R&D activity by foreign subsidiaries in its country and 0 if otherwise. In many countries, the government influences foreign R&D activity by means of various positive and negative inducements. Positive inducements can take the form of tax subsidies, for example. More effective, however, seem to be negative inducements such as price controls, exchange controls, import or export restrictions, or patent protection. We expect to see a positive relationship between host country restrictions on R&D and the incidence of joint R&D in our sample. Table 5–2 summarizes the variables that might affect the incidence of R&D activity in U.S.-foreign joint venture subsidiaries.

Empirical Results

Since only the presence or absence of R&D activity was observable for the newly formed joint ventures in our sample, it was necessary to use a qualitative choice model such as probit or logit to estimate the effects of the various explanatory variables on joint R&D. The use of probit, logit, or other statistical techniques for dealing with binary choice problems is an area of econometrics that has received a great deal of attention in the last 10 years. The use of these statistical techniques has proved to be particularly important in analyzing firm behavior. In analyzing the behavior of the firm, the often unquantifiable nature of the activity under observation or the lack of available data can generate the yes/no types of variables found in this research.

The difference between probit and logit, the two most commonly used binary choice estimators, is usually quite small. This research uses probit analysis. In this case, the probability that R&D = 1 is assumed to be a function of the form $\beta_0 + \beta_1 X_1 + \ldots \beta_n X_n$, distributed as the cumulative distribution function for the standard normal distribution.[5]

In the first test, a probit model was estimated over the sample of joint ventures formed by U.S. firms and foreign partners between 1974 and 1982. All nine explanatory variables were included. For one of these variables, *USRDS*, only 334 out of 420 observations were available. The model was, therefore, estimated over this reduced sample of 334 joint ventures. The probit maximum likelihood estimates for the probability of joint R&D activity are as given in table 5–3. The correlation matrix for the independent variables is given in table 5–4.

Table 5–3
Probit Estimates of the Determinants of Joint Venture R&D Activity, 1974–1982 Data

Independent Variable	Estimated Coefficient	Standard Error	t-Statistic
C (intercept)	−2.810	0.328	−8.578
POP	0.137E−02	0.745E−03	1.836
INTL	0.405	0.225	1.799
INDRD	0.158	0.440E−01	3.583
FTECH	1.162	0.241	4.829
FPARTNER	0.650	0.232	2.802
GDPC	0.575E−01	0.259E−01	2.225
USRDS	−2.032	2.594	−0.784
MES	−0.151E−02	0.102E−02	−1.473
GOVT	−0.502E−01	0.222	−0.227

Dependent variable: *RD*
Number of observations: 334
Mean of dependent variable: .15
Number of R&D joint ventures: 49
Number of non-R&D joint ventures: 285
$\chi^2(8) = 185.2$

Table 5–4
Correlation Matrix for R&D Equation with 334 Observations

	RD	*C*	*POP*	*INTL*	*INDRD*
RD	1.000				
C	0.000	0.000			
POP	−0.004	0.000	1.000		
INTL	0.280	0.000	−0.095	1.000	
INDRD	0.271	0.000	0.033	0.106	1.000
FTECH	0.391	0.000	−0.063	0.305	0.057
FPARTNER	0.280	0.000	−0.081	0.241	0.122
GDPC	0.269	0.000	−0.200	0.159	0.149
USRDS	0.115	0.000	0.025	0.080	0.409
MES	0.054	0.000	0.022	0.029	0.574
GOVT	0.043	0.000	0.189	−0.034	0.092

X², R², and Other Measures of Goodness of Fit

Overall, the model does fairly well in identifying some of the important determinants of joint R&D activity. As a measure of the significance of the model as a whole, the likelihood ratio test is used to test the null hypothesis that the set of estimated coefficients are all insignificantly different from zero. This test is given by the statistic − 2 times the log of the likelihood ratio, which is distributed as χ^2 with 8 degrees of freedom. At $\chi^2 = 185.2$, we can reject the null hypothesis and state that the equation is statistically significant at better than the 99 percent level.

In addition, one might want to measure the goodness of fit of the model. Unfortunately, for qualitative choice models like the probit model estimated here, there is no truly satisfactory measure for the degree of fit. This analysis presents two measures that researchers have occasionally used. The first is based on calculating a statistic analogous to Theil's R^2 in a standard regression model. The second, a measure more frequently used in discriminant analysis, is based on the number of right and wrong predictions generated by the estimated model. These and other measures have various deficiencies that will be noted. Together, however, they provide some additional insight into the model's overall explanatory power.

The R^2 statistic is calculated from the sum of squared residuals:

$$R^2 = 1 - \frac{\sum_{i=1}^{n} (RD_i - \widehat{RD}_i)^2}{\sum_{i=1}^{n} (RD_i - \overline{RD})^2}$$

FTECH	FPARTNER	GDPC	USRDS	MES	GOVT
1.000					
0.092	1.000				
0.205	0.399	1.000			
0.091	0.110	0.097	1.000		
0.007	−0.039	−0.040	0.166	1.000	
−0.010	0.215	0.221	0.049	0.035	1.000

where

$$\overline{RD} = n^{-1} \sum_{i=1}^{n} RD_i$$

Correcting for degrees of freedom, we can calculate Theil's R^2 as follows:

$$\overline{R}^2 = 1 - n^{-1}(n-K)(1-R^2)$$

where n is the sample size (334) and K is the number of unknown parameters in the model (10).

At $\overline{R}^2 = .34$, there is still a large amount of variation in the likelihood of joint R&D that is not explained by the model. Unfortunately, as concluded by Amemiya, we do not have enough experience with the use of R^2 in qualitative choice models to be able to say whether there is some bias on these estimates. Morrison, for example, explains how an upper bound can exist on R^2 when calculated for qualitative choice models.[6] It is possible, therefore, that the results presented here are actually better than they appear when compared against an upper bound of less than the usual limit of $R^2 = 1$. Goldberger, however, provides a counterargument, claiming that Morrison's results are based on a special case where the predictor is distributed in a particular way.[7] Goldberger concludes that in most cases, the proper upper bound is still $R^2 = 1$.

An alternative method of measuring the model's explanatory power is to check the number of observations in which the model correctly predicts the presence or absence of joint R&D. An estimated probability, $\widehat{RD} = .50$, is typically chosen as the cutoff. If $\widehat{RD} \geq .50$ and joint R&D

actually occurs for that observation, or $\widehat{RD} < .50$ and joint R&D does not occur, we classify that observation as being correctly predicted by the model.

For the model estimated in table 5–3, the model correctly predicts the presence or absence of joint R&D in 293 out of 334 observations, a success rate of 88 percent. The distribution of estimated probabilities for R&D and non-R&D joint ventures is graphed in figures 5–1 and 5–2.

There are two clear difficulties with using the correct classification method. First is the issue of what constitutes the appropriate cutoff to classify an observation as a correct or incorrect prediction. We have chosen $\widehat{RD} = .50$. One might feel, however, that an estimated probability around 50 percent is a good predictor of neither the presence nor absence of R&D. The predictor is said to be ambiguous. One might wish to set stricter limits on what constitutes a good prediction. Table 5–5 shows how the model does at different cutoffs. As can be seen, the model does relatively well even when the estimated probability of R&D has to be greater than or equal to 75 percent to predict correctly the presence of R&D and less than 25 percent to predict correctly its absence.

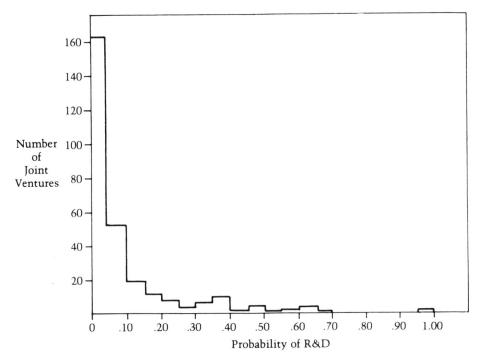

Figure 5–1. Distribution of Estimated Probabilities when Actual Joint Venture R&D Activity = 0 (No R&D)

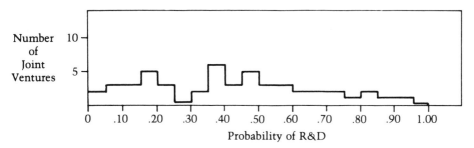

Figure 5–2. Distribution of Estimated Probabilities when Actual Joint Venture R&D Activity = 1 (R&D)

Another difficulty is that in cases where an event happens with either relatively high or low probabilities, most models do well by the correct classification criterion.[8] Joint R&D is a relatively infrequent occurrence in our sample. Out of 334 observations, only 49 had joint R&D (14.7 percent). Indeed, figures 5–1 and 5–2 show that the estimated probabilities across the sample are primarily concentrated at the very low end of the sample.

Due to some of the difficulties associated with both the R^2 statistic for a qualitative choice model and the correct classification criterion, one cannot make a definitive statement about the goodness of fit of the model. It appears, however, that under either method, the model does not do too badly. An $\bar{R}^2$ of .34 is in line with estimates on pooled cross-sectional data of this sort. As was mentioned before, however, it is clear that there are other, though perhaps unquantifiable, variables that might affect the joint R&D decision. By the correct classification method, the model has a success rate of greater than 75 percent even at relatively strict cutoffs on what constitutes a correct prediction. This figure also supports the viability of our model, though the danger of an upward bias due to the low frequency of joint R&D in the sample needs to be kept in mind.

Coefficient Estimates and t-Statistics

Turning to the individual coefficient estimates on the independent variables, it appears that several of the variables in the model have a significant influence on the likelihood of joint R&D activity. The coefficients on *POP, INTL, INDRD, FTECH, FPARTNER,* and *GDPC* are significantly different from zero at the 95 percent confidence level or better. *MES* is significant at the 90 percent confidence level.[9]

The joint venture's decision to undertake R&D activity, therefore, appears to be responsive to some of the same factors that can influence

Table 5–5
Comparison of the Observed and Expected Incidence of Joint Venture Activity

X/Y	Number Correctly Specified		Error Rate		Number Ambiguous	
50%/50%	294	(88%)	40	(12%)	—	
60%/40%	281	(84%)	30	(9%)	23	(7%)
75%/25%	254	(76%)	17	(5%)	63	(19%)

Notes: At $\widehat{RD_i} \geq X$, the model predicts the presence of joint venture R&D. If $RD = 1$, the prediction is correct.

At $\widehat{RD_i} < Y$, the model predicts the absence of joint venture R&D. If $RD = 0$, the prediction is correct.

R&D in autonomous firms. These factors include market size, a technically competitive industry environment, access to technical know-how (through the foreign partner in this case), and the local availability of scientists, technicians, and R&D facilities and equipment. There is also some indication that the joint venture's R&D activities may be constrained by the interrelationship between its operations and those of its parent firms. The U.S. parent's expertise in R&D activity or scale economies in R&D operations may constrain the joint venture's involvement in R&D operations, centralizing them in the parent's facilities instead.

The positive and significant coefficients on *POP* and *INTL* and perhaps *GDPC* indicate the effect of market size on innovative activity. The size of the host country market as well as the joint venture's presence in international markets can increase the expected rate of return on R&D activities and hence the likelihood of the joint venture's pursuing R&D. The industry R&D/Sales ratio (*INDRD*) and the technical ability of the foreign partner (*FTECH*) also have a positive and highly significant effect on the likelihood of joint venture R&D. The positive and significant coefficient on *GDPC* reflects the potential importance of a country environment on the decision to establish R&D operations and perhaps the effect of market size, as above.

MES has a negative effect on the likelihood of joint R&D even though it is significant at only the 90 percent confidence level. We find, therefore, some evidence in this result of the interrelationship between the joint venture and its parent firm and the effect this interrelationship has on joint venture behavior. If economies of scale in R&D are high, the parent firm may very well find it more profitable to centralize R&D in one location—most typically, at the parent firm's home country in its own facilities.

The high positive correlation between *MES* and *INDRD*, however causes some difficulty in disentangling the independent effect of *MES* on joint R&D from that of *INDRD*. Because *MES* is negatively related to joint R&D and *INDRD* is positively related, multicollinearity may drive the estimates toward zero. One might suspect, therefore, that *MES*, on its own, could exert an even stronger negative influence on joint R&D than is reported here. When *INDRD* is dropped from the model, *MES* does, in fact, pick up a lot of its effect. Its sign changes from negative to positive with a resulting *t*-statistic of 1.11. When *MES* is dropped from the model, *INDRD* likewise captures some of the negative effect of *MES*. The estimated coefficient drops by one standard deviation from 0.158 to 0.115, though the *t*-statistic stays fairly constant.

Turning to the variables for which there are alternative hypotheses about their effect on joint R&D, we get some interesting results. The coefficient on *FPARTNER* is positive and highly significant. Hence, a joint venture with a strong foreign partner appears to encourage R&D, perhaps because it implies access to a larger market, consisting of a larger set of countries. The alternative hypothesis suggested that U.S. firms would be reluctant to share technology with strong foreign partners. The notion was that a strong partner could use this technology for its own competitive advantage and perhaps to the future detriment of the U.S. firm. U.S. firms might, therefore, be hesitant to become involved in collaborative R&D because of this risk. It appears, however, that despite this potential risk, the benefit of market access is the stronger effect.

The coefficient on *USRDS* is negative though insignificant. The standard error on the coefficient prevents us from inferring too much from these results. It is, however, interesting to see that the most R&D-intensive U.S. parent firms are not the most likely to support R&D in their foreign joint venture subsidiaries. It appears that R&D-intensive U.S. parents might find it more profitable to conduct R&D themselves and thus be less inclined to encourage R&D in their foreign joint venture subsidiaries.[10]

As was the case with the coefficient estimate on *MES*, however, *USRDS* is highly positively correlated with *INDRD*. It is therefore possible that multicollinearity is mixing the two effects. Dropping *INDRD* from the model does change the sign on *USRDS* from negative to positive with a *t*-statistic of .696. This implies that when both *INDRD* and *USRDS* are included in the same equation, the independent effect of *USRDS* on joint R&D is intertwined with the strong positive effect of *INDRD*.

As a further attempt to gain some insight into the relationship between *USRDS* and joint R&D, the model was re-estimated, controlling for the interaction between *USRDS* and *FTECH*. The hypothesis was that if both the U.S. firm and the foreign partner were technically skilled, collaborative R&D would be more mutually attractive. Neither partner would be contributing all the technical skills and resources, and both could benefit from the other partner's know-how. A new variable, *INTER*, was therefore formed as the product of *FTECH* and *USRDS* for values of *USRDS* greater than the sample mean ($INTER = FTECH \times USRDS$, $USRDS \geq 0.032$). Hence, *INTER* controls for joint ventures between two technically endowed partners.

The results of this estimation are presented in table 5–6. *INTER* is positive as hypothesized and significant at the 90 percent confidence level. It is interesting that the independent effect of *USRDS*, controlling for those cases where both partners are technically endowed, is now more pronounced. The coefficient on *USRDS* is negative and significant at the 90 percent confidence level. This conforms with the previous hypothesis that R&D-intensive parents may find it more profitable to conduct R&D themselves and suggests that this might be especially so when the flow of technology to the joint venture would be one-sided.

The final variable in our model, *GOVT*, is estimated with the opposite sign from what was expected and is insignificant. The positive correlation between *GOVT* and several of the other independent variables may indicate multicollinearity problems in isolating the effect of *GOVT*

Table 5–6
Probit Estimates of the Determinants of Joint R&D Activity, Controlling for the Interaction between *FTECH* and *USRDS*, 1974–1982 Data

Independent Variable	Estimated Coefficient	Standard Error	t-Statistic
C (intercept)	− 2.781	0.333	− 8.343
POP	0.146E − 02	0.760E − 03	1.924
INTL	0.405	0.227	1.784
INDRD	0.167	0.457E − 01	3.647
FTECH	0.970	0.274	3.546
FPARTNER	0.684	0.236	2.918
GDPC	0.602E − 01	0.260E − 01	2.324
USRDS	− 6.546	4.601	− 1.423
MES	− 0.149E − 02	0.103E − 02	− 1.454
GOVT	0.850E − 02	0.228	0.374E − 01
INTER	7.573	5.202	1.456

Dependent variable: *RD*
Number of observations: 334
Mean of dependent variable: .15
Number of R&D joint ventures: 49
Number of non-R&D joint ventures: 285
$\chi^2 = 182.9$

alone. *GOVT* is positively correlated with *POP*, *FPARTNER*, and *GDPC*. Since *GOVT* is very loosely proxied by joint venture location in Japan, France, Brazil, or Mexico, correlations with these other variables are not surprising and may account for some of the lack of precision in this estimate. *GOVT* was dropped from the equation to see what effect this would have on the coefficients and standard errors of the remaining variables. The coefficients and standard errors were hardly affected at all, implying that weak data and not multicollinearity are probably the main source of the poor results for this variable.[11]

The source of difficulty with the *GOVT* variable lies largely with the data. The particularly weak data on different government policies toward the R&D activity of foreign investors reflect the difficulty of obtaining this type of information. This proxy variable controls for the joint venture being formed in any one of the four countries that Behrman and Fischer found to offer specific inducements to foreign R&D activity.[12] Since the study covered far fewer countries than the 56 countries spanned by the database used in this research, important omissions may have occurred. It is also possible that government policies may have changed from before and after 1978 (the year in which the survey was taken), making a static proxy variable an inappropriate measure over time.

Empirical Results over 420 Observations

The empirical results presented in this chapter have been estimated over a subsample of 334 out of a total 420 observations on joint venture activity because only 334 observations were available for the *USRDS* variable. Since the coefficient on *USRDS* was not statistically significant in any of the preceding estimates, the model was re-estimated over the entire 420 observations, excluding *USRDS*, to see whether the results would change. The results over the entire sample are given in table 5–7.

The estimated coefficients are not significantly different from those reported in table 5–3 for the reduced sample. All remain within one standard error of the original estimates given in table 5–3. The $\bar{R}^2$, however, has dropped from .34 to .29, indicating some loss of explanatory power in dropping *USRDS* from the equation or possibly an increase in unexplained variance resulting from the introduction of new observations. *MES* drops somewhat in significance and is no longer significant at the 90 percent confidence level.

These results alleviate one concern that exists whenever analyzing results based on a subsample of the data; namely, one needs to consider whether the subsample is representative of the whole sample environment or whether one has introduced bias into the model by choosing a particular subset of the data to analyze. The results presented here do

Table 5–7
Probit Estimates of the Determinants of Joint Venture R&D Activity,
Excluding *USRDS*, 1974–1982 Data

Independent Variable	Estimated Coefficient	Standard Error	t-Statistic
C (intercept)	− 2.728	0.280	− 9.738
POP	0.167E − 02	0.607E − 03	2.754
INTL	0.432	0.191	2.259
INDRD	0.127	0.352E − 01	3.613
FTECH	0.956	0.203	4.711
FPARTNER	0.588	0.194	3.023
GDPC	0.643E − 01	0.227E − 01	2.829
MES	− 0.936E − 03	0.895E − 03	− 1.045
GOVT	− 0.238	0.197	− 0.211

Dependent variable: *RD*
Number of observations: 420
Mean of dependent variable: .15
Number of R&D joint ventures: 62
Number of non-R&D joint ventures: 358
$\chi^2(7) = 249.8$
$\bar{R}^2 = .29$

not indicate a problem along these lines. It seems that the greater error would be in leaving *USRDS* out of the model and, hence, to risk biasing the results by misspecifying the equation.

Constancy of the Model over Time

The model was re-estimated to consider the possibility of a significant shift in the estimated coefficients over time. The structural relationships in the model could be affected by changes in the type of R&D being done in overseas joint venture subsidiaries or by changes in the amount of control that U.S. firms are able to exercise over joint venture subsidiaries or choose to exercise. The notion of structural change was formally examined by comparing the values of the coefficients for the first part of the sample with those generated for the latter part of the sample.

The decision to split the sample into 1974–1979 and 1980–1982 data was primarily based on data considerations. This resulted in 182 observations in the first half of the sample, including 20 R&D joint ventures, and 152 observations in the second half, including 29 R&D joint ventures. The alternative was to split the sample after 1978. This, however, would have yielded 139 observations in the first period, with only 11

R&D joint ventures. Given the high degree of diversity among observations and the relatively large number of explanatory variables on R&D limiting the degrees of freedom, this split was a problem. With only 11 R&D observations, the estimates would be too sensitive to the vagaries of any one observation.

Furthermore, the reasons for structural change appear to be gradual shifts in the nature of the R&D being done in foreign joint ventures and in the relationship between U.S. parents and joint venture subsidiaries. There thus does not appear to be a natural break in the sample—as if a new law, for example, were passed in a given year that accounted for the structural change in the model. Where estimates were calculated between the first and second halves of the sample, however, they were redone to check if an earlier cutoff at 1978 would have made a significant difference. In most cases, it did not. Where it did, the difference is noted in the text.

The Entire Model

Tables 5–8 and 5–9 present the coefficient estimates and their t-statistics for 1974–1979 data and 1980–1982 data. A comparison of the log likelihood ratios of the two subsamples of the data with the entire sample tests whether the combination of all changes in the estimated coefficients

Table 5–8
Probit Estimates of the Determinants of Joint Venture R&D, 1974–1979 Data

Independent Variable	Estimated Coefficient	Standard Error	t-Statistic
C (intercept)	− 2.007	0.482	− 4.164
POP	− 0.102E–01	0.707E – 02	− 1.449
INTL	− 0.176	0.380	− 0.463
INDRD	0.314	0.897E – 01	3.502
FTECH	0.975	0.407	2.393
FPARTNER	0.674	0.336	2.007
GDPC	0.408E – 01	0.335E – 01	1.218
USRDS	− 3.115	3.504	− 0.889
MES	− 0.685E – 02	0.252E – 02	− 2.718
GOVT	0.687	0.549	1.251

Dependent variable: *RD*
Number of observations: 182
Mean of dependent variable: .11
Number of R&D joint ventures: 20
Number of non-R&D joint ventures: 162
$\chi^2(8)$ = 83.6

Table 5–9
Probit Estimates of the Determinants of Joint Venture R&D,
1980–1982 Data

Independent Variable	Estimated Coefficient	Standard Error	t-Statistic
C (intercept)	– 4.190	0.832	– 5.039
POP	0.245E – 02	0.989E – 03	2.476
INTL	0.929	0.388	2.394
INDRD	0.153	0.669E – 01	2.294
FTECH	1.492	0.359	4.150
FPARTNER	0.745	0.380	1.961
GDPC	0.889E – 01	0.554E – 01	1.625
USRDS	– 0.916	3.843	– 0.238
MES	0.105E – 02	0.141E – 02	0.742
GOVT	0.204E – 02	0.348	0.585E – 02

Dependent variable: *RD*
Number of observations: 152
Mean of dependent variable: .19
Number of R&D joint ventures: 29
Number of non-R&D joint ventures: 123
$\chi^2(8) = 83.7$

are significant. With $\chi^2 = 17.82$, the null hypothesis that the model has remained constant throughout the time period of our sample can be rejected at the 97.5 percent confidence level.[13]

The Individual Estimates

To estimate structural change for each of the explanatory variables in the model, a dummy variable, *LT*, to signify "later" years, was created. *LT* was set equal to 0 from 1974 through 1979 and to 1 from 1980 through 1982. Each of the explanatory variables as well as the constant term was then multiplied by *LT* to yield 10 more variables. A test of the coefficients on these new variables tests the hypothesis that each coefficient has remained constant throughout the time period of our sample. These estimates are given in table 5–10.

Three variables appear to exhibit a statistically significant shift in their effect on the likelihood of joint R&D. The first two, *POP* and *INTL*, change from having a negative, though insignificant, effect on joint R&D to a positive, significant effect in the last three years of the sample. One explanation for the shift in the coefficients of *POP* and *INTL* might be that more important, innovative R&D is starting to be done in overseas joint venture subsidiaries relative to less expensive, adaptive types of R&D that used to prevail. U.S. MNEs might be undertaking more

Table 5-10
Probit Estimates of the Determinants of Joint R&D Activity,
Testing for Structural Change between 1974–1979 Data
and 1980–1982 Data

Independent Variable	Estimated Coefficient	Standard Error	t-Statistic
C (intercept)	− 2.007	0.482	− 4.164
LTC	− 2.183	0.961	− 2.272
POP	− 0.102E − 01	0.707E − 02	− 1.449
LTPOP	0.127E − 01	0.714E − 02	1.778
INTL	− 0.176	0.380	− 0.463
LTINTL	1.105	0.543	2.035
INDRD	0.314	0.897E − 01	3.502
LTINDRD	− 0.161	0.112	− 1.437
FTECH	0.975	0.407	2.393
LTFTECH	0.517	0.543	0.951
FPARTNER	0.674	0.336	2.007
LTFPARTNER	0.711E − 01	0.507	0.140
GDPC	0.408E − 01	0.335E − 01	1.218
LTGDPC	0.491E − 01	0.647E − 01	0.759
USRDS	− 3.115	3.504	− 0.889
LTUSRDS	2.200	5.201	0.423
MES	− 0.685E − 02	0.242E − 02	− 2.718
LTMES	0.790E − 02	0.289E − 02	2.733
GOVT	0.687	0.549	1.251
LTGOVT	− 0.685	0.650	− 1.054

Dependent variable: *RD*
Number of observations: 334
Mean of dependent variable: .15
Number of R&D joint ventures: 49
Number of non-R&D joint ventures: 285
$\chi^2(18) = 167.37$

joint overseas R&D as a substitute for rather than as a minor addition to home-based R&D efforts. If this is so, expected market demand might be more of a consideration when undertaking such larger-scale R&D operations.

MES is the third variable whose coefficient has undergone a significant shift. Over the 1974–1979 data, it exerted a negative and significant effect on joint R&D activity. Over the 1980–1982 data, however, it was positive though insignificant. This would be consistent with more U.S. MNEs locating major R&D facilities abroad as a substitute for home-based R&D efforts in certain product lines. High *MES* in R&D might still imply centralization of R&D efforts, though this centralization may now be occurring in overseas joint venture locations for some products.

The shift in the *MES* coefficient may also reflect changes in the types of joint ventures being formed. Specifically, one can imagine that the size of the joint venture might affect the amount it would be willing to invest in R&D operations (as a certain percentage of net sales, for example). If the average size of joint venture subsidiaries increased from the first to the second part of the sample, more joint ventures might be large enough to invest in minimum efficient scale R&D operations.

For the other variables in our model, the results are inconclusive. While the results do not reject the equality hypothesis at the 95 percent confidence level, there does appear to be some possibility of a structural shift. The estimated coefficients on *FTECH*, *FPARTNER*, and *GDPC* are larger in the latter years of our sample. If joint ventures were deciding to do more important, innovative R&D, the technical skills of the foreign partner, its market access, and the scientific climate of the host country might indeed become more of a factor in the decision to establish R&D operations.[14] Similarly, the R&D intensity of the U.S. parent firm may make joint R&D more likely rather than deter it as joint ventures take on more product responsibility. The estimated coefficient on *USRDS*, though still negative, does in fact get much smaller and less significant as a deterrence to joint R&D in the 1980–1982 data.

Two variables, however, do not change as might be expected. If joint ventures were exerting more autonomous control over their product lines and product development, we should expect to see a larger estimated coefficient on *INDRD*. Instead, the magnitude of this coefficient halves, though it remains positive and significant. Similarly, the coefficient on *GOVT* undergoes a puzzling shift. Between the early and latter years of the sample, it changes from the expected positive effect to an insignificant effect. It is possible that the countries that used to offer specific inducements to foreign R&D activity no longer do so to the same extent. The weak data on this variable, however, have already been discussed, preventing us from inferring too much from this result.

Determinants of the Increasing Incidence of Joint R&D Activity

The empirical results presented can be used to address one of the questions posed by this research: Why has the percentage of international joint ventures with R&D operations increased so much in the latter part of our sample?

The first explanation is that more international joint ventures are taking place in countries, industries, and among parent firms more favorably related to the profitable pursuit of R&D. An increase in certain variables that are positively associated with joint R&D or a decrease in certain variables negatively associated with joint R&D could bring about this effect. A change in the sample environment may thus be contributing to the increasing incidence of R&D activity in recent U.S.-foreign joint ventures.

The second explanation is that the model describing the decision to undertake joint R&D has somehow changed over time. This could be due to changing U.S. parent joint venture relationships or a change in the type of R&D being done in overseas joint venture subsidiaries. In this case, a structural change in the model may make the likelihood of joint R&D more responsive to the certain country-, industry-, and firm-specific variables described earlier.

The Sample Environment versus Structural Changes in the Model

The relevant question is the importance of structural change relative to changes in the environment in explaining the increase in joint R&D in recent years. To address this question, it is possible to partition the change in R&D into a shift in the coefficients and a shift in the values of the exogenous variables. For the 1974–1979 data, coefficients that maximized the likelihood of joint R&D observed in our sample were estimated. Data from this first part of the sample multiplied by these coefficients yield the mean value estimate of R&D in the 1974–1979 period, as is represented in equation (5.1):

$$\overline{RD}_{74-79} = \hat{\alpha}_{74-79} = \hat{\beta}_{1,\,74-79}POP_{74-79} \ldots + \hat{\beta}_{n,\,74-79}GOVT_{74-79} \quad (5.1)$$

Similarly, over the latter period, 1980–1982, the mean value estimate of R&D is given in equation (5.2):

$$\overline{RD}_{80-82} = \hat{\alpha}_{80-82} + \hat{\beta}_{1,\,80-82}POP_{80-82} \ldots + \hat{\beta}_{n,\,80-82}GOVT_{80-82} \quad (5.2)$$

By substituting data on the explanatory variables from the 1980–1982 period into equation (5.1), one can get some idea of the pure effect of changes in the sample environment on joint R&D. Hence, equation (5.3) yields a new fitted value of R&D somewhere in between the actual values observed in the first period, 1974–1979, and in the second period, 1980–1982:

$$\overline{RD}_{\Delta SMPL} = \hat{\alpha}_{74-79} + \hat{\beta}_{1,\,74-79}POP_{80-82} \ldots + \hat{\beta}_{n,\,74-79}GOVT_{80-82} \quad (5.3)$$

By keeping the sample environment the same but changing the structural coefficients, one can similarly isolate the pure effect of structural change on the likelihood of joint R&D. Equation (5.4) shows how this estimate can be constructed:

$$\overline{RD}_{\Delta COEF} = \hat{\alpha}_{80-82} + \hat{\beta}_{1,\,80-82}POP_{74-79} \ldots + \hat{\beta}_{n,\,80-82}GOVT_{74-79} \qquad (5.4)$$

The estimates derived from equations (5.3) and (5.4) are compared with the actual mean value estimates of R&D in 1974–1979 and 1980–1982 in table 5–11. The estimates presented in table 5–11 indicate that changes in the sample environment are the prime force behind the increasing incidence of joint R&D. The pure effect of these changes accounts for 76 percent of the difference between the mean value estimate of R&D between 1974 and 1979 and the mean value estimate of R&D between 1980 and 1982. The pure effect of structural·change is insignificant, even slightly contrary to the trend. It is important to keep in mind, however, the interaction between structural change and environment change over time that makes up the additional distance in table 5–11. Hence, structural change may still be somewhat important in its interactive capacity in affecting the increase in joint R&D. It seems safe to say, however, that changes in the sample environment exhibit the much stronger effect in our model.

Changes in the Sample Environment Conducive to Joint R&D

The empirical results have identified certain variables that appear to affect significantly the likelihood that a new joint venture will become involved in joint R&D operations. It is, therefore, possible that certain key variables that are positively associated with joint R&D have become more prevalent over time in our sample. Similarly, it is possible that variables that exert a negative influence on the likelihood of joint R&D have become less frequent in the sample. This hypothesis is readily addressed by considering the characteristics of the sample environment

Table 5–11
Changes in the Sample Environment Relative to Structural Changes in the Model

$\widehat{RD}$ (Data$_{1974-1979}$; Coefficients$_{1974-1979}$)	= .10989
$\widehat{RD}$ (Data$_{1974-1979}$; Coefficients$_{1980-1982}$)	= .09583
$\widehat{RD}$ (Data$_{1980-1982}$; Coefficients$_{1974-1979}$)	= .17127
$\widehat{RD}$ (Data$_{1980-1982}$; Coefficients$_{1980-1982}$)	= .19070

over time. Table 5–12 presents the mean values of the explanatory variables in the model for each of the 9 years in the sample period.

Among those variables found to be significant in explaining the likelihood of joint R&D, several variables appear to have followed distinct trends from the beginning to the latter years of the sample. The percentage of joint ventures serving international markets (*INTL*) appears to have increased over time. The mean R&D/Sales ratio of the industries in which joint ventures are being formed (*INDRD*) also appears to be increasing. Also, the percentage of joint ventures where the foreign partner contributes product or process technology to the joint venture (*FTECH*) has similarly increased. Since these three variables have been found to be positively associated with the likelihood of joint R&D, their increasing characterization of the sample environment should at least partially explain the increasing presence of joint ventures involved in collaborative R&D activity.

Table 5–13 presents the coefficients of the explanatory variables converted to indicate the magnitude of the effect that a unit increase in the explanatory variable would have on the expected probability of joint R&D in the sample. *INDRD* and *FTECH* have had the greatest effect on the increase in joint R&D, while *POP* has had the largest negative effect (though a change in the structural coefficient on *POP* over time has countered this latter effect). The increasing proportion of international joint ventures in high-technology industries may stem from a number of economic and political factors: industry shakeouts in many R&D-intensive industries,

Table 5–12
Mean Values of Dependent and Independent Variables in R&D Model for 334 Observations

	1974	1975	1976	1977	1978	1979	1980	1981	1982	1974–1982
Dependent variable										
RD	0.10	0.00	0.05	0.06	0.17	0.21	0.22	0.15	0.21	0.15
Independent variables										
POP	68.60	55.99	61.01	69.21	43.66	59.63	88.24	71.50	141.1	77.0
INTL	0.22	0.33	0.23	0.29	0.25	0.35	0.53	0.49	0.38	0.37
INDRD	2.70	2.50	4.24	2.39	4.25	3.14	3.36	4.20	4.44	3.51
FTECH	0.04	0.07	0.36	0.06	0.13	0.19	0.24	0.20	0.24	0.17
FPARTNER	0.35	0.15	0.36	0.29	0.38	0.40	0.38	0.44	0.43	0.37
GDPC	6.30	5.01	7.77	6.76	6.51	6.27	5.61	6.71	7.69	6.46
USRDS	0.030	0.019	0.033	0.018	0.033	0.026	0.031	0.039	0.047	0.032
MES	117.1	150.3	163.9	65.8	126.4	132.8	123.9	133.9	123.7	127.7
GOVT	0.35	0.37	0.45	0.42	0.21	0.40	0.20	0.31	0.45	0.34

Table 5–13
Effects of Changes in Explanatory Variables over Time on the Likelihood of Joint Venture R&D Activity

Variable	$Mean_{74-79}$	$Mean_{80-82}$	Δ	$Coefficient_{74-79}$	Effect ($\Delta \times Coefficient$)
POP	60.462	96.796	36.334	−0.00113	−0.041
INTL	0.280	0.474	0.194	−0.01929	−0.004
INDRD	3.137	3.963	0.826	0.03453	0.029
FTECH	0.132	0.224	0.092	0.10715	0.010
FPARTNER	0.330	0.414	0.084	0.07411	0.006
GDPC	6.350	6.583	0.233	0.00449	0.001
USRDS	0.027	0.038	0.011	−0.34233	−0.004
MES	127.819	127.456	−0.363	−0.00075	0.000
GOVT	0.363	0.309	−0.054	0.07554	−0.004

leading to consolidation among several U.S. and foreign competitors; the rising cost and pace of R&D; and increasing protectionism in many advanced countries, particularly in high-technology sectors.

The growing number of technically skilled foreign partners in our sample also appears consistent with various macro trends in the global competitive environment. Over the last decade, many foreign firms have succeeded in narrowing the technology gap in certain high-technology industries. In part, this has been due to (1) the high levels of foreign private and government expenditures on R&D compared to levels of spending in the United States and (2) the increasing foreign technological concentration on creating products for the world market rather than for domestic customers alone. Technical know-how has thus often been much more evenly balanced between U.S. and foreign joint venture partners than in the past.

Finally, as we have seen, market size of the host country, as proxied by population, has increased from the beginning to the latter years of the sample. The reason behind this change may stem in part from changing host government regulations concerning foreign investment and foreign competition in host markets. Some large industrialized European countries, for example, have become increasingly protectionist and nationalist concerning their choice between local and foreign suppliers. In many cases, joint venture participation has become a necessity for foreign firms seeking access to lucrative yet chauvinistic markets. French government protectionism of several high-technology industries is a good example. This protectionism may increase the percentage of joint ventures being formed in large countries, increasing the mean value of *POP* in our sample.

Other countries, such as Japan and China, starting from a highly protectionist climate for foreign investment, have eased restrictions on foreign exchange and foreign investment. This has made it easier for foreign firms to set up subsidiaries or joint ventures in those countries. In particular, the number of joint ventures formed in China since 1979 may have contributed to the higher values of *POP* in the latter part of the sample.

A larger database would, of course, be necessary to address these issues rigorously. Data on wholly owned subsidiaries, for example, would be necessary to differentiate between those forces affecting international joint venture formation and forces affecting other types of international investment as well. The discussion here suggests some hypotheses to pursue.

It is possible that some of the changes in the sample environment reflect a change in the types of joint ventures being formed. If the assumption that the various characteristics of the joint venture are fixed is relaxed, one could test the simultaneous determination of certain joint venture characteristics. The choice of joint venture location, for example, may be influenced by the type of joint venture planned, like whether or not R&D will be done. Similarly, the decision to export may be determined along with the decision to do R&D, as in the development of new products for global markets. Simultaneous testing of this sort is complicated by the lack of appropriate instrumental variables for many of the variables in our model. Nevertheless, in chapter 6, we use the empirical results on the determinants of joint venture activity along with the empirical results presented in this chapter to construct a simultaneous model of joint venture R&D and export determination.

Summary

Chapter 5 focuses on collaborative R&D activity in U.S.-foreign joint venture subsidiaries. It considers the effects of various country-, industry-, and firm-specific variables on the likelihood that the joint venture will become involved in R&D operations of its own. It further tests whether the influence of these variables has changed much over time. The results are used to analyze the increasing percentage of U.S.-foreign joint ventures involved in joint R&D operations. By 1982, about 20 percent of newly formed U.S.-foreign joint ventures each year were involved in some type of collaborative R&D activity.

The joint venture's decision to undertake R&D activity appears to be responsive to some of the same factors that can influence R&D in autonomous firms. In addition, however, its decision is also influenced by the interrelationship between the joint venture's activities and the profit-maximizing objectives of its parent firms. Probit estimates were used to test the effects of these factors on joint R&D in a sample of 334 U.S.-foreign joint ventures formed between 1974 and 1982.

Several variables appear to have a significant influence on the likelihood of joint R&D activity. The variables that appear to have a positive effect on joint R&D are (1) market size, including both domestic and international markets; (2) a technically competitive industry environment; (3) partnership with a technically skilled foreign partner; (4) market access through the foreign partner's international distribution network; and (5) the general technical environment of the host country (local availability of scientists, technicians, R&D facilities, and equipment). The variables that appear to exert a negative influence on joint R&D are (6) scale economies in R&D operations and (7) the R&D intensity of the U.S. parent firm, especially when the foreign partner does not contribute technology to the joint venture. This latter effect indicates that U.S. R&D-intensive parents may find it more profitable to conduct R&D themselves and suggests that this might be especially true when the flow of technology to the joint venture would be one-sided.

Notes

1. J. Schmookler, *Invention and Economic Growth* (Cambridge: Harvard University Press, 1966).

2. E. Mansfield, A. Romeo, and S. Wagner, "Foreign Trade and U.S. Research and Development," *Review of Economics and Statistics*, February 1979, pp. 49–57.

3. H.G. Grabowski and N.D. Baxter, "Rivalry in Industrial Research and Development," *Journal of Industrial Economics*, Vol. 22, 1973, pp. 209–235.

4. Jack N. Behrman and William A. Fischer, *Overseas R&D Activities of Transnational Companies* (Cambridge, Mass.: Oelgeschlager, Gunn & Hain, Publishers, Inc., 1980), p. 82.

5. For more information on the use of probit, logit, or other qualitative response models, see T. Amemiya, "Qualitative Response Models: A Survey," *Journal of Economic Literature*, December 1981, pp. 1483–1536.

6. Donald G. Morrison, "Upper Bounds for Correlations Between Binary Outcomes and Probabilistic Predictions," *Journal of the American Statistical Association*, March 1972, pp. 68–70.

7. Arthur S. Goldberger, "Correlations Between Binary Outcomes and Probabilistic Predictions," *Journal of the American Statistical Association*, March 1973, p. 84.

8. Amemiya, "Qualitative Response Models," p. 1504.

9. Two-tailed tests were used for variables with alternative sign predictions (*FPARTNER* and *USRDS*). Otherwise, a one-tailed test was employed.

10. This result was examined to see whether diversification made a difference. In particular, the idea was that the R&D intensity of the U.S. parent

might only constrain joint venture R&D operations when the joint venture and parent belonged to the same industry. If the joint venture operated in another industry outside of the U.S. parent's field of expertise, the results could change. When the model was re-estimated, however, similarity or dissimilarity between joint venture and parent operations did not have a significant effect.

11. The model was also re-estimated controlling for the effect of *GOVT* on joint R&D, but only in high R&D/Sales industries. The notion was that host governments would be more active in encouraging R&D in high-technology industries than in relatively low-technology sectors (the mean industry R&D/Sales ratio was taken as the cutoff). While the coefficient was estimated with the correct sign (positive), however, it was still insignificant.

12. Behrman and Fischer, *Overseas R&D Activities.*

13. This result holds as well when the sample is split one year earlier. In that case, $\chi^2(8) = 19.4$ and the null hypothesis can be rejected at an even greater level of certainty.

14. When the sample was split one year earlier at 1978, the coefficients on these three variables were even larger in the second half of the sample. For *FPARTNER* and *GDPC*, the change was significant at the 90 percent level.

6
The Determinants of Export Activity by U.S.-Foreign Joint Ventures

I n seeking to identify some of the determinants of joint venture export activity, this research draws on the industrial organization literature that has documented the effects of various country-, industry-, and firm-specific factors on the export behavior of the multinational firm. The literature, however, has almost totally been concerned with the export decision of an autonomous firm. This research tests these relationships in the more complex case of a joint venture, whose behavior is affected not only by its own profit-maximizing objectives but also by the profit-maximizing objectives of its parent firms and the role that the joint venture plays in their international strategies.

The results are used to analyze the significant increase in the percentage of U.S.-foreign joint ventures being formed to serve international markets. Table 6–1 shows how the percentage of joint ventures with export operations has changed between 1974 and 1982. By the last 3 years of the sample, about half of the international joint ventures being formed each year were intending to compete in both domestic and export markets. This trend is in contrast to the earlier years of the sample when the majority of joint ventures were formed to serve the local market alone. It is also in contrast to the literature that has characterized traditional joint ventures as being fairly localized within their host countries.

Variables and Hypotheses

The first objective of this chapter is to identify the country, industry, and firm-specific variables which may affect the likelihood of export activity in our sample. The sources of data are given in the appendix. Unfortunately, the data are such that we only know if the joint venture is involved in export operations and not the countries to which it is exporting. Thus, comparative variables between the exporting and importing countries such as differences in factor endowments and technology as well as price and income effects are necessarily absent from the model.

Table 6–1
Export Activity in U.S.-Foreign Joint Ventures

Joint Ventures	1974	1975	1976	1977	1978	1979	1980	1981	1982	Total
Number with exports	14	10	7	8	6	20	38	35	24	162
Number in sample	64	29	28	23	28	54	72	68	54	420
Percent of total	22	34	25	35	21	37	53	51	44	39

However, the dataset is rich enough to provide information on the joint venture's activities, including the industry in which the joint venture competes, the joint venture's functional activities, and the characteristics of the foreign partner. This information allows us to test other similarly important relationships that have been largely ignored in the empirical literature for lack of data.

Minimum Efficient Scale in Production (MES–PCN)

MES–PCN represents the minimum efficient scale of production activities in the joint venture's industry. In certain industries, high fixed costs or declining marginal costs in manufacturing will increase the productive capacity needed to operate efficiently. Joint ventures formed in such industries may be more likely to seek export markets as a way of extending the market and thus allowing for the exploitation of scale economies. Krugman demonstrates how trade may be caused by economies of scale instead of the usual differences in technology or factor endowments emphasized in the literature.[1] Given the positive effect of production economies of scale on the likelihood of joint venture exports, we should expect a positive coefficient on this variable.

Population (POP)

The *POP* variable represents the population of the foreign country in which the joint venture is based. The size of the host country markets, as proxied by the population of that country, is expected to have a negative impact on the likelihood that the joint venture seeks export markets. The lumpiness of the investment that is usually necessary to set up a new joint venture subsidiary may make it efficient for the joint venture to serve a larger market than the host market alone. The high search and negotiation costs involved in establishing a new joint venture, for example, may not pay off for a small country market unless that market is supplemented by additional export sales.

The effect this variable attempts to capture is really much broader than the interaction between host market size and economies of scale in production.[2] It includes the market's ability to support start-up costs, as mentioned earlier, administrative infrastructures, as well as efficient scale in the various functional activities of the joint venture, including manufacturing, R&D, and marketing. For this reason, *POP* is introduced separately from *MES–PCN*. *POP* is expected to be negatively related to the joint venture's involvement in export operations.

Marketing-Related Intangible Assets

The presence of intangible assets is normally linked with a firm's propensity to pursue international markets. The ratio of a firm's selling expenditure to net sales, including both media and nonmedia expenditures, can be an indication that the firm possesses important intangible assets such as a well-known company or brand name or a reputation for quality among its customers. The transactions costs literature would then argue that the market failures associated with arm's-length transactions in intangible assets may make it more profitable for the firm to sell to foreign markets itself than to sell the assets to foreign producers. Williamson describes some of the difficulties of buying or selling the rights to intangible assets.[3] The difficulties in buying or selling intangibles may include assigning a value to image, the uncertainty of not knowing how well the image will be translated into a new geographic market, and the problems of divulging marketing secrets while in the process of negotiations.

In trying to determine the likelihood of export activity for an individual joint venture, it would be optimal to know the media and nonmedia selling expenditures for the joint venture. Since these data are not available, we assume that the distribution of marketing intensities among the joint ventures in our sample can be approximated by the average marketing intensities of the joint venture industries.

Media Expenditure/Sales (MEDIA)

MEDIA is the ratio of media advertising expenditures to net sales for the joint venture industry. The media advertising intensity of the joint venture may exert either a positive or a negative effect on the likelihood of joint venture exports. As discussed, media advertising expenditures are one way in which a firm may build brand name reputation and recognition. It is possible, therefore, that joint ventures in high media/sales industries would be more inclined to seek export markets. This would enable them to capitalize on the intangible assets acquired through their advertising efforts.

In contrast, the rent-seeking motive may be countered by the country-specificity of the product in this case. The high media/sales industries in our sample are typically industries such as cigarettes, cosmetics, chewing gum, and other food products. These industries often require adaptation to local market tastes and preferences. Caves and Khalilzadeh-Shirazi, for example, found that for the United States there is a negative relationship between the trade intensity of an industry and the advertising outlays as a percentage of sales for that industry.[4] Similarly, Caves et al. found industry advertising outlays as a percentage of sales to be a negative predictor of the importance of import competition in Canadian markets.[5]

For autonomous firms operating in these industries, the rent-seeking motive has more typically been accommodated by direct investment rather than export penetration into a foreign market. In the case of a joint venture subsidiary, however, the effect may be to limit the joint venture's activities to the domestic market. Even though exports may be profitable for the joint venture, the parent firm may find it more profitable to serve other foreign markets on its own by establishing local subsidiaries there rather than by exporting from the joint venture. Hence, profit-maximizing behavior for the parent is not necessarily profit-maximizing for the joint venture.

For these reasons, there may be a negative relationship between industry media advertising intensity and joint venture export activity. On balance, however, there is no sign prediction.

Nonmedia Selling Expenditure/Sales (NONMEDIA)

The *NONMEDIA* variable is the ratio of nonmedia selling expenditures to net sales for the joint venture's industry. Nonmedia expenditures along with media expenditures make up the firm's total selling expenditures. Nonmedia expenditures could include factors such as the firm's outlays on its sales force, nonmedia promotional devices (such as catalogs, exhibits, displays, or temporary price reductions for promotional purposes), or marketing administration and market research. Examples of high nonmedia/sales industries in our sample cover a diverse group of industries including computers, medical instruments, and food and beverage products such as bakery goods, coffee, and soft drinks.

Nonmedia sales promotion may indicate the presence of intangible assets that may encourage the joint venture's rent-seeking entry into export markets. Nonmedia expenditures are also likely to reflect intrinsic product heterogeneity, requiring the seller to provide a substantial amount of information directly to the buyers of the product and perhaps other auxiliary services as well. Intrinsic heterogeneities plus associated scale economies would thus imply a limited number of world production sites and a greater likelihood of exporting from any one producer. We might, therefore, expect a positive relationship between joint ventures in high nonmedia sales promotion industries and the likelihood of joint venture export activity.

R&D (RD)

The *RD* dummy variable is equal to 1 if the joint venture is involved in R&D operations and 0 if otherwise. Other types of intangible assets that have been positively linked with a firm's expansion into foreign markets are those associated with a firm's technical know-how. A number of studies have shown R&D intensity to be a significant determinant of export activity, including Horst[6] and Swedenborg.[7] Patented processes or designs or technical skills may enable a firm to reap profits on those assets in foreign markets. Again, market failures associated with selling the assets may make it more profitable to sell the goods embodying these assets instead. Hence, we should expect to see a positive relationship between joint R&D and the likelihood that the joint venture has export operations.

A specification problem arises at this point in that, as was shown in the previous chapter, *RD* is determined in part by *INTL*, the dependent variable in this model. Given the strength of prior theoretical and empirical research delineating the causal relationship of R&D on entry into international markets, however, one might expect *RD* to have a positive effect on *INTL*, even correcting for simultaneous equation bias. This problem is addressed rigorously in a later section by specifying a two-equation model where *RD* and *INTL* are simultaneously determined.

U.S. Parent's Foreign Subsidiary Sales/Net Sales (USSUB)

The *USSUB* variable represents the ratio of the U.S. parent firm's foreign subsidiary sales to net sales. There are reasons to believe that the international orientation of the U.S. parent firm may exert either a positive or a negative influence on the likelihood of joint venture export operations. The facility with which a joint venture can access foreign export markets depends in part on the particular distribution channels and marketing know-how at its disposal. If the U.S. parent has an extensive network of international operations and makes them available to the joint venture, the joint venture might be more likely to undertake export activity. Similarly, it may be able to capitalize on the experience of the U.S. parent in competing in foreign countries. Under these circumstances, we should expect to see a positive relationship between *USSUB* and the likelihood of joint venture export activity.

Conversely, there is also the potential for conflict between the U.S. parent firm's existing or planned activities in foreign markets and the joint venture's desire to target these same markets for export. The joint venture's decision to export to those markets could mean that the U.S. parent might end up competing against itself. Under these circumstances, one can hypothesize that the greater the U.S. parent firm's foreign sales to net sales, the more likely for such conflict to occur. Hence, *USSUB* might be negatively associated with joint venture export activity.

The empirical results indicate which of these two influences has the dominant effect. The next section considers also whether similarity or dissimilarity between the U.S. parent's and the joint venture's product lines affects these results.

Foreign Partner (FPARTNER)

The *FPARTNER* dummy variable is set equal to 1 if the foreign partner operates in international markets outside of its home market and is set equal to 0 if there is no indication of international scope. The effects here are potentially the same as those described for *USSUB*. If, on the other hand, the foreign partner has access to international markets, its know-how or its distribution network might help the joint venture's export activities. Hence, we might expect a positive relationship between *FPARTNER* and joint venture exports. On the other hand, the potential for conflict exists when the joint venture's products are most similar or central to the foreign partner's product line. The empirical results will again give us some indication of the relative strengths of these two effects.

Joint Venture Located in EEC (EEC)

The *EEC* dummy variable is set equal to 1 if the joint venture is based in a country that is a member of the European Economic Community (EEC) and 0 if otherwise. Tariffs and other import barriers can impede otherwise profitable export operations. While it was impossible to control for this effect uniformly throughout the database, the EEC is one block of countries within which intercountry trade may be facilitated to a greater degree than among other countries in the sample. Other research has found EEC membership to be a significant determinant of export activity, reflecting the advantage that EEC members have in exporting to other countries in the EEC.[8] If intercountry trade within the EEC is, in general, subject to fewer trade impediments than among other countries in our sample, we might expect a positive relationship between the variable *EEC* and joint venture export activity.

Table 6–2 summarizes the variables that are expected to influence the likelihood of the joint venture's pursuing export operations.

Table 6–2
Expected Effect of Variables on the Incidence of Export Activity by U.S.-Foreign Venture Subsidiaries

Variable	Expected Sign
MES-PCN	+
POP	−
MEDIA	+ or −
NONMEDIA	+
RD	+
USSUB	+ or −
FPARTNER	+ or −
EEC	+

Empirical Results

A probit model was estimated to test the effects of the various country-, industry-, and firm-specific variables on the likelihood that the joint venture will seek export markets. Probit rather than ordinary least squares estimation was necessary because of the dichotomous nature of the dependent variable. We are only able to observe whether or not the joint venture actually undertakes export activity. Hence, *INTL* takes the value 1 when the joint venture intends to export some of its product and 0 otherwise.

The estimates are based on a reduced sample of 284 out of 420 available observations on joint venture activity in our database. The sample was constrained by the limited availability of data on the foreign operations of the U.S. parent firms, *USSUB* (see the appendix for details). Despite this constraint, however, the number of observations was still sufficiently large to enable testing. The results for the reduced sample were not significantly different from the results obtained when *USSUB* was dropped from the equation and the model re-estimated over 420 observations.

The maximum likelihood estimates for the probability that the joint venture will seek export markets are reported in table 6–3. The correlation matrix is presented in table 6–4 as a check on the multicollinearity of the exogenous variables in the model.

X^2, R^2, *and Other Measures of Goodness of Fit*

Overall, the model does quite well in identifying some of the important factors affecting joint venture export activity. The likelihood test is used to test the null hypothesis that the set of estimated coefficients are all insignificantly different from zero. At $\chi^2 = 338.30$, we can reject the null hypothesis and state that the model is statistically significant at

Table 6–3
Probit Estimates of the Determinants of Joint Venture Export Activity,
1974–1982 Data

Independent Variable	Estimated Coefficient	Standard Error	t-Statistic
C (intercept)	−0.635	0.219	−2.898
MES-PCN	6.130	3.368	1.820
POP	−0.11E−02	0.719E−03	−1.400
MEDIA	−0.879E−01	0.525E−01	−1.676
NONMEDIA	0.214E−01	0.208E−01	1.028
RD	0.590	0.239	2.474
USSUB	−0.517	0.514	−1.006
FPARTNER	0.378	0.172	2.202
EEC	0.360	0.187	1.925

Dependent variable: *INTL*

Number of observations: 284

Mean of dependent variable: .37

Number of export joint ventures: 106

Number of nonexport joint ventures: 178

$\chi^2(7) = 338.3$

better than the 99 percent confidence level (the 99 percent critical value for $\chi^2(8)$ is 20.09).

In addition, one might want to measure the goodness of fit of the model. Unfortunately, as we discussed in chapter 5, there is no truly satisfactory measure for goodness of fit for qualitative choice models. As an approximation, one can calculate a statistic analogous to Theil's R^2 in a standard regression model. For the model estimated in table 6–3, $\bar{R}^2 = .15$, indicating a large amount of variation not explained by the model. As discussed in chapter 5, however, there is some question as to whether this result might be biased.

As an alternative method of measuring the model's explanatory power, we can check the number of observations in which the model correctly predicts the presence or absence of joint venture export activity. An estimated probability, $INTL = .50$, is typically chosen as the cutoff. If $\widehat{INTL} \geq .50$ and $INTL = 1$, meaning that the model estimates the likelihood of export activity for the observation at greater than or equal to 50 percent and the joint venture actually does export, we classify that observation as being correctly predicted by the model. Similarly, if $\widehat{INTL} < .50$ and $INTL = 0$, we also count this as a correct prediction. For the model estimated in table 6–3, the model correctly predicts the presence or absence of joint venture export activity in 197 out of 284 observations, a success rate of approximately 69 percent. Table 6–5 shows how the model does at different cutoffs.

As can be seen, the explanatory power of the model drops off sharply as the cutoffs become more restrictive as to what constitutes a good prediction. Nevertheless, the predictive power of the model appears to be fairly good, considering the necessary omission of comparative variables such as factor endowments and price and income effects between importing and exporting countries. The distribution of the estimated probabilities for the actual cases where the joint venture does not undertake export activity and where it does are graphed in figures 6–1 and 6–2.

Coefficient Estimates and t-Statistics

The results are, in general, consistent with the hypotheses presented in the previous section. *MES-PCN, RD, FPARTNER,* and *EEC* are significantly different from zero at the 95 percent confidence level or better. *POP* and *MEDIA* are statistically significant at the 90 percent level.[9] The correlation matrix indicates that multicollinearity is not a major problem in the model.

For the variables for which there were conflicting hypotheses about their effects on export activity, some interesting results emerge. The coefficient on *MEDIA* is negative and significant at the 90 percent confidence level. It would thus appear that despite the intangible assets created by media advertising expenditures, the country-specificity of products in these industries may discourage joint venture export activity. As was hypothesized earlier, the parent firm may find it more profitable to serve other foreign markets by establishing local subsidiaries in these markets rather than by exporting from the joint venture.

In contrast, where intangible assets appear to be created by non-media selling efforts, the country-specificity of the product does not appear to be as large a counterforce to export activity. Hence, the positive, though insignificant, coefficient on *NONMEDIA* may be caused by the joint venture's desire to capitalize on these intangible assets by exporting to foreign markets.

The positive and significant coefficient on *FPARTNER* indicates that the foreign firm's international distribution channels and know-how encourage joint venture exports. The negative coefficient on *USSUB*, however, supports the motion that the U.S. parent firm may find joint venture export activity in conflict with its other operations. The joint venture's use of its parent firm's foreign distribution channels and know-how may be constrained by the parent firm's desire to keep potential export markets for itself. In that sense, the joint venture's ability to act on a profit-seeking motive may be very different from an analysis of an autonomous firm.

Table 6–4
Correlation Matrix for Variables Affecting the Likelihood
of Joint Venture Export Activity

	INTL	*C*	*MES-PCN*	*POP*	*MEDIA*
INTL	1.000				
C	0.000	0.000			
MES-PCN	0.081	0.000	1.000		
POP	−0.105	0.000	−0.000	1.000	
MEDIA	−0.075	0.000	0.289	0.008	1.000
NONMEDIA	0.052	0.000	−0.080	−0.021	0.339
RD	0.232	0.000	0.008	0.006	−0.033
USSUB1	0.151	0.000	0.063	−0.060	−0.126
USSUB	−0.060	0.000	0.214	0.061	0.163
FPARTNER	0.238	0.000	0.079	−0.017	−0.081
EEC	0.198	0.000	0.012	−0.140	0.064

[a]*USSUB1* controls for joint ventures in industries other than their U.S. parent firm's primary operations. *USSUB1* is introduced later in the chapter.

Effect of U.S. Parent Exports on Joint Venture
Export Activity

Since the potential for conflict appears to be highest when the parent firm and the joint venture market the same product (in that case, the joint venture and parent are potential competitors in third country markets), we can control for this in the data and see what effect it has on the sign of *USSUB*.[10] The hypothesis is that potential parent–joint venture competition—particularly competition in an important product line—impedes joint venture export activity. In contrast, where the U.S. parent may not be as threatened by joint venture competition—that is, where the joint venture markets dissimilar or peripheral product lines—the U.S. parent's marketing know-how and distribution channels in these countries may encourage rather than discourage joint venture export activity.

To test this hypothesis, a new variable, *D1* is constructed. *D1* divides the data into those joint ventures that compete in the same industry as the U.S. parent firm's primary operations and those that do not. This is done by comparing the joint venture's industry SIC code with the primary SIC code of the U.S. parent firm and seeing whether at the two-digit level, the SIC codes are the same. *USSUB1* is then generated as in table 6–6 to control for the effect of different or peripheral product lines on the U.S. parent firm's desire to constrain joint venture expansion into export markets.

The model is re-estimated to see whether the effect of *USSUB1* is significantly different from *USSUB* in explaining the likelihood of joint venture export activity. The results are given in table 6–7. The results

NONMEDIA	RD	USSUB1[a]	USSUB	FPARTNER	EEC
1.000					
0.160	1.000				
−0.056	0.044	1.000			
0.063	0.001	0.240	1.000		
0.011	0.277	0.135	−0.059	1.000	
0.090	0.217	0.067	−0.003	0.236	1.000

appear to support the proposed hypothesis. *USSUB1* is positive and significant at the 97.5 percent confidence level. We should, therefore, expect that joint ventures producing a different product line from the U.S. parent firm or one peripheral to the parent's primary product line should be less constrained in their ability to pursue export markets than joint ventures producing the same product line.

The model was also re-estimated to control for whether the joint venture produced a product in any of the U.S. parent's two-digit SIC industries (up to seven industries were checked for each U.S. parent firm). The motivation was to account for any potential conflict between the joint venture's export operations and the U.S. parent firm's foreign operations, whether or not they were in its primary product line. It was thought

Table 6–5
Comparison of the Observed and Expected Incidence of Joint Venture Export Activity

X/Y	Number Correctly Specified		Error Rate		Number Ambiguous	
50%/50%	197	(69%)	87	(31%)	—	
60%/40%	157	(55%)	55	(19%)	72	(25%)
75%/25%	63	(22%)	20	(7%)	201	(71%)

Notes: At $\widehat{INTL}_i \geq X$, the model predicts the presence of joint venture exports. If $INTL = 1$, the prediction is correct.

At $\widehat{INTL}_i < Y$, the model predicts the absence of joint venture exports. If $INTL = 0$, the prediction is correct.

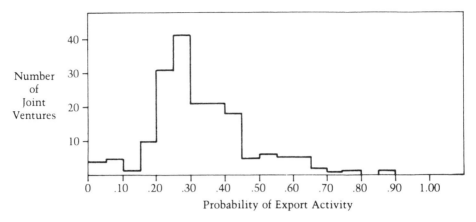

Figure 6–1. Distribution of Estimated Probabilities when Actual Joint Venture Export Activity = 0 (No Exports)

possible, for example, that diversified firms with several important product lines might resist joint venture export activity in any of these industries.

Unfortunately, data on U.S. parent firm SIC codes were only available for the most recent year, 1982, rather than for each of the sample years, 1974–1982. This was not considered to be a problem at the primary SIC code level and hence in the construction of $D1$ since a firm's main product line will probably not change much over time. When checking all the

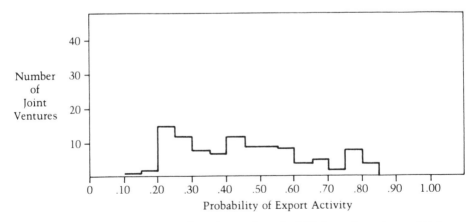

Figure 6–2. Distribution of Estimated Probabilities when Actual Joint Venture Export Activity = 1 (Exports)

Table 6–6
Effects of Similar versus Dissimilar Product Lines between Joint Venture and U.S. Parent Firms

Variable	Description	Expected Sign
D1	Dummy variable	
USSUB1	USSUB1 × D1	+
USSUB	As before	−

parent firm's industries, however, there might be substantial change over 9 years. For this reason, when a joint venture was matched with one of the parent firm's SIC industries in 1982, this might not necessarily mean that the parent firm was actually in that industry in the year the joint venture was formed. Redundancy was also a potential problem in that joint venture operations might be included in the list of parent firm industries.

Keeping in mind the drawbacks of the data, this measure of diversification was tested, and the results were presented in table 6–8. $USSUB2 = D2 \times USSUB$, where $D2 = 1$ when the joint venture is in a different two-

Table 6–7
Probit Estimates of the Determinants of Joint Venture Export Activity, Controlling for Dissimilarity between Joint Venture Industry and Primary SIC Industry of U.S. Parent Firm, *USSUB1*, 1974–1982 Data

Independent Variable	Estimated Coefficient	Standard Error	t-Statistic
C (intercept)	− 0.652	0.229	− 2.847
MES-PCN	5.583	3.368	1.658
POP	− 0.103E − 02	0.798E − 03	− 1.285
MEDIA	− 0.731E − 01	0.523E − 01	− 1.398
NONMEDIA	0.243E − 01	0.211E − 01	1.151
RD	0.605	0.240	2.519
USSUB1	1.392	0.625	2.229
USSUB	− 1.053	0.643	− 1.637
FPARTNER	0.337	0.173	1.950
EEC	0.349	0.188	1.861

Dependent variable: *INTL*

Number of observations: 284

Mean of dependent variable: .37

Number of export joint ventures: 106

Number of nonexport joint ventures: 178

$\chi^2(8) = 333.3$

Table 6–8
Probit Estimates of the Determinants of Joint Venture Export Activity, Controlling for Dissimilarity between Joint Venture Industry and All SIC Industries of U.S. Parent Firm, *USSUB2*, 1974–1982 Data

Independent Variable	Estimated Coefficient	Standard Error	t-Statistic
C (intercept)	−0.641	0.224	−2.860
MES-PCN	5.798	3.366	1.723
POP	−0.108E−02	0.790E−03	−1.370
MEDIA	−0.836E−01	0.524E−01	−1.595
NONMEDIA	0.209E−01	0.209E−01	1.002
RD	0.611	0.240	2.541
USSUB2	0.971	0.713	1.362
USSUB	−0.684	0.568	−1.203
FPARTNER	0.359	0.172	2.081
EEC	0.357	0.187	1.906

Dependent variable: *INTL*
Number of observations: 284
Mean of dependent variable: .37
Number of export joint ventures: 106
Number of nonexport joint ventures: 178
$\chi^2(8) = 336.4$

digit industry from any of the U.S. parent firm's operations and 0 if there is a match. While the difference is not as pronounced as for *USSUB1*, the coefficient on *USSUB2* is still positive and significant at the 90 percent confidence level.

Constancy of the Model over Time

To test for any structural variation in the model over time, the model is re-estimated, controlling for whether the data were generated in the first or the second part of the sample. The dummy variable, *LT* (late), takes the value 0 from 1974 to 1979 and 1 from 1980 to 1982. Ten new variables are then formed by multiplying *LT* by the explanatory variables and the constant term in the model. The new estimates are given in table 6–9. Tables 6–10 and 6–11 give the coefficient estimates when the model is run for the 1974–1979 data and then for the 1980–1982 data.

As a measure of the constancy of the whole model, the log likelihood ratio test was used. This tests the null hypothesis that none of the estimated coefficients is significantly different from zero. At $\chi^2(8) = 22.50$, we can reject the null hypothesis of constancy at the 99 percent confidence level (the 99 percent critical value for $\chi^2(8)$ is 20.09).

Table 6–9
Probit Estimates of the Determinants of Joint Venture Export Activity, Testing for Structural Change between 1974–1979 Data and 1980–1982 Data

Independent Variable	Estimated Coefficient	Standard Error	t-statistic
C (intercept)	−0.769	0.326	−2.359
LTC	0.693	0.483	1.435
MES-PCN	3.219	5.460	0.590
LTMES-PCN	2.945	7.251	0.406
POP	−0.703E−02	0.301E−02	−2.333
LTPOP	0.605E−02	0.313E−02	1.931
MEDIA	−0.612E−01	0.863E−01	−0.710
LTMEDIA	−0.206E−01	0.111	−0.185
NONMEDIA	0.263E−01	0.290E−01	0.907
LTNONMEDIA	−0.105E−01	0.451E−01	−0.235
RD	−0.635E−01	0.388	−0.164
LTRD	0.970	0.526	1.842
USSUB1	1.640	0.944	1.738
LTUSSUB1	−0.482	1.288	−0.374
USSUB	0.492E−01	0.632	0.778E−01
LTUSSUB	−2.370	1.126	−2.104
FPARTNER	0.517	0.269	1.919
LTFPARTNER	−0.205	0.367	−0.559
EEC	0.246	0.275	0.894
LTEEC	0.219	0.396	0.553

LT signifies 1980–1982 data.
Dependent variable: *INTL*
Number of observations: 284
Mean of dependent variable: .37
Number of export joint ventures: 106
Number of nonexport joint ventures: 178
$\chi^2(18) = 310.8$

The *t*-distribution tests whether the change in each of the coefficients is statistically significant over time. Three variables exhibit a statistically significant shift in their effect on the likelihood of joint venture export activity: *POP, RD,* and *USSUB.*

The negative effect of *POP* as a determinant of joint venture export activity diminishes significantly from the first to the second part of the sample. Between 1980 and 1982 the population of the host country becomes a much weaker influence on the joint venture's decision to export. The estimated coefficient drops from −0.0070 to −0.0010 from the first to the second half of the sample and is no longer statistically significant at even the 90 percent confidence level (though it is still significant at the 80 percent level).

Table 6–10
Probit Estimates of the Determinants of Joint Venture Export Activity,
1974–1979 Data

Independent Variable	Estimated Coefficient	Standard Error	t-Statistic
C (intercept)	-0.769	0.326	-2.359
MES-PCN	3.219	5.460	0.590
POP	$-0.703E-02$	$0.301E-02$	-2.333
MEDIA	$-0.612E-01$	$0.863E-01$	-0.710
NONMEDIA	$0.263E-01$	$0.290E-01$	0.907
RD	$-0.635E-01$	0.388	-0.164
USSUB1	1.640	0.944	1.738
USSUB	$0.492E-01$	0.632	$0.778E-01$
FPARTNER	0.517	0.269	1.919
EEC	0.246	0.275	0.894

Dependent variable: *INTL*
Number of observations: 147
Mean of dependent variable: .28
Number of export joint ventures: 41
Number of nonexport joint ventures: 106
$\chi^2(8) = 154.4$

One possible explanation for this change has to do with the increasing percentage of joint ventures with export operations in the sample environment. While a firm might not put a home market subsidiary in a small market, it can put an export subsidiary in either a small or a large market. In the first part of the sample, when the majority of joint ventures was home market subsidiaries, the negative and statistically significant coefficient on *POP* reflected the tendency for these home market subsidiaries to be located in large markets. In the second half of the sample, when only half of the joint ventures were home market subsidiaries and half were export subsidiaries, the ambiguous effect of *POP* in the latter case weakens the statistical significance of this variable.

The effect of joint R&D on the joint venture's decision to export has also changed significantly between the early and the latter part of the sample. Between 1974 and 1979, the joint venture's involvement in R&D operations had an insignificant effect on exports. From 1980 to 1982, however, the coefficient on *RD* increased from -0.064 to 0.906 and became significant at the 95 percent confidence level.

One explanation for this dramatic shift in explanatory power may be related to actual changes in the types of R&D that joint ventures have been pursuing in these later years. As discussed in the previous chapter, U.S.-foreign joint ventures appear to be becoming increasingly involved in more basic types of product or process development than they have in the past. Adaptive R&D, which may have been more prevalent in the ear-

Table 6–11
Probit Estimates of the Determinants of Joint Venture Export Activity,
1980–1982 Data

Independent Variable	Estimated Coefficient	Standard Error	t-Statistic
C (intercept)	−0.758E−01	0.357	−0.212
MES-PCN	6.164	4.771	1.292
POP	−0.984E−03	0.848E−03	−1.161
MEDIA	−0.818E−01	0.700E−01	−1.168
NONMEDIA	0.157E−01	0.346E−01	0.455
RD	0.906	0.356	2.549
USSUB1	1.158	0.875	1.323
USSUB	−2.321	0.932	−2.489
FPARTNER	0.311	0.250	1.247
EEC	0.465	0.285	1.629

Dependent variable: *INTL*
Number of observations: 137
Mean of dependent variable: .47
Number of export joint ventures: 65
Number of nonexport joint ventures: 72
$\chi^2(8) = 156.3$

lier part of the sample, may not have been as transferable to other foreign markets or so expensive as to necessitate a larger market over which to spread costs. More costly and basic types of R&D, conversely, might cause the joint venture to seek larger, even global, markets for the R&D-embodying product.

The third variable whose effect on joint venture export activity appears to have changed over time is *USSUB*. Table 6–9 shows *USSUB* as exerting a stronger negative effect over time, with the estimated coefficient changing from 0.05 (insignificant) to −2.32 (highly significant) between the early and latter years of the sample. U.S. parent firms with high ratios of foreign sales to net sales thus appear to be exerting a strong negative influence on joint venture exports when the joint venture competes in the same primary SIC industry as the parent firm.

The reasons behind this shift are unclear. It is possible that as joint ventures become more powerful competitive entities, their presence in third country markets would more significantly interfere with parent firm operations in those countries. It is also possible that highly international U.S. parent firms have become more capable of profitably serving these markets themselves as transportation and communications costs have declined. More U.S. firms have also begun adopting global strategies requiring the coordination and full control of worldwide operations wherever possible.

Determinants of the Increasing Incidence of Joint Venture Export Activity

Having identified some of the key country-, industry-, and firm-specific factors affecting the joint venture's decision to seek export markets, we can now address the question of why joint venture export activity has increased over time.

Sample Environment Changes

The empirical tests have analyzed the effects of several variables on the incidence of joint venture export activity. Table 6–12 presents the mean values of these explanatory variables for each of the 9 years in our sample.

Only two variables appear to have changed significantly from the beginning to the latter years of the sample: *RD* and *USSUB1*. Both variables were found to be positively associated with the joint venture's decision to undertake export operations. To check the magnitude of the effect of these and other changes in the explanatory variables on the dependent variable, however, we need to recalculate the probit coefficients. Table 6–13 shows how the change in the values of the explanatory variables from the first part to the second part of the sample has affected the expected probability of joint venture export activity.

None of the changes in the values of the explanatory variables appears to have caused a particularly large effect on *INTL*. An increase in the value of *RD* and *USSUB1*, however, has contributed the most to an increase in *INTL*. An increase in *POP* (negatively related to *INTL*) has provided the most counterforce to this trend.

Table 6–12
Mean Values of Dependent and Independent Variables in Model

	1974	1975	1976	1977	1978	1979	1980	1981	1982	1974–1982
Dependent variable										
INTL	0.21	0.35	0.21	0.39	0.25	0.30	0.53	0.51	0.37	0.37
Independent variables										
MES-PCN	0.029	0.021	0.019	0.023	0.021	0.016	0.025	0.027	0.022	0.023
POP	78.38	55.81	61.75	71.06	41.51	56.82	81.26	71.02	139.45	78.31
MEDIA	1.55	1.18	1.29	1.56	0.87	1.12	1.75	1.40	1.01	1.33
NONMEDIA	6.41	6.47	7.26	7.26	7.57	6.52	6.95	7.35	7.49	7.06
RD	0.091	0.000	0.053	0.056	0.150	0.216	0.213	0.130	0.190	0.140
USSUB	0.289	0.199	0.191	0.173	0.259	0.247	0.242	0.258	0.244	0.241
USSUB1	0.044	0.056	0.026	0.071	0.081	0.097	0.079	0.109	0.127	0.084
FPARTNER	0.364	0.200	0.368	0.389	0.350	0.378	0.383	0.426	0.372	0.370
EEC	0.044	0.056	0.026	0.071	0.081	0.097	0.079	0.109	0.127	0.084

Table 6–13
Effects of Changes in Explanatory Variables over Time
on the Likelihood of Joint Venture Export Activity

Variable	$Mean_{74-79}$	$Mean_{80-82}$	$\triangle$	$Coefficient_{74-89}$	Effect ($\triangle \times Coefficient$)
MES-PCN	0.022	0.025	0.003	2.08366	0.006
POP	61.820	96.009	34.189	– 0.00038	– 0.013
MEDIA	1.268	1.399	0.131	– 0.02729	– 0.004
NONMEDIA	6.884	7.256	0.372	0.00905	0.003
RD	0.109	0.175	0.066	0.22568	0.015
USSUB1	0.065	0.104	0.039	0.51952	0.020
USSUB	0.235	0.248	0.013	– 0.39305	– 0.005
FPARTNER	0.347	0.394	0.047	0.12597	0.006
EEC	0.265	0.263	– 0.002	0.13039	– 0.000

Structural Change

In comparison, we measured the effects of structural change in the model against the effects that these changes in the environment have in explaining the increase in joint venture export activity in recent years. We have already seen that some degree of structural change has occurred in the model over time. Here we are interested in defining the relative importance of this effect.

Similar to the analysis in chapter 5, we partition the change in *INTL* into the change caused by a shift in the exogenous variables and the change caused by a shift in the coefficients. Table 6–14 estimates these effects. To isolate the effect of changes in the sample environment, the model was estimated using the structural coefficients from the first part of the sample (1974–1979) and data from the second part of the sample (1980–1982). To isolate the effect of structural changes in the model, the estimates were run using the coefficients from the second part of the sample (1980–1982) and data from the first part (1974–1979).

While both a change in the sample environment and a structural change in the model appear to account for some of the increase in joint venture export activity, the structural change is by far the dominant ef-

Table 6–14
Changes in the Sample Environment Relative to Structural Changes in the Model

$\widehat{INTL}$ (Data$_{1974-1979}$; Coefficients$_{1974-1979}$) = .279

$\widehat{INTL}$ (Data$_{1980-1982}$; Coefficients$_{1974-1979}$) = .299

$\widehat{INTL}$ (Data$_{1974-1979}$; Coefficients$_{1980-1982}$) = .456

$\widehat{INTL}$ (Data$_{1980-1982}$; Coefficients$_{1980-1982}$) = .474

Table 6–15
Effects of Structural Change over Time on the Likelihood of Joint Venture Export Activity

Variable	$Coef_{74-79}$	$Coef_{80-82}$	$\triangle$	$Mean_{74-79}$	Effect ($\triangle \times$ Mean)
MES-PCN	0.898	2.925	2.027	0.022	0.045
POP	−0.002	−0.000	0.002	61.820	0.124
MEDIA	−0.017	−0.039	−0.022	1.268	−0.028
NONMEDIA	0.007	0.007	0.000	6.884	0.000
RD	−0.018	0.430	0.448	0.109	0.049
USSUB1	0.458	0.550	0.092	0.065	0.006
USSUB	0.014	−1.101	−1.115	0.235	−0.262
FPARTNER	0.144	0.148	0.004	0.347	0.001
EEC	0.069	0.220	0.151	0.265	0.040

fect. It is possible to estimate the magnitude of the individual effects of structural change in each of the estimated coefficients on the likelihood of joint venture export activity. These results are given in table 6–15.

Export Activity and R&D as Simultaneously Determined Joint Venture Characteristics

The single-equation estimation techniques used have assumed that the explanatory variables are all fixed, exogenous influences. However, certain variables that act as determinants of joint venture export activity may be determined in part by planned entry into export markets. In particular, chapter 5 showed that joint R&D activity is related to the expected market size and, hence, to both domestic and export market participation. This chapter has described how the possession of intangible technical assets, acquired through R&D activity, is an impetus in itself on joint venture exports.

The simultaneous interaction between joint venture R&D and export activity can be modeled in a manner analogous to two-stage least squares estimation. The use of this technique for discrete rather than continuous dependent variables was proposed by Maller.[11]

Equations (6.1) and (6.2) are the structural relationships in which we are interested, with RD^* and $INTL^*$ being the true latent variables underlying the model:

$$RD^* = \gamma_1 INTL^* + \beta_1' X_1 + u_1 \tag{6.1}$$

$$INTL^* = \gamma_2 RD^* + \beta_2' X_2 + u_2 \tag{6.2}$$

The reduced form of the system is shown in equations (6.3) and (6.4), where RD^* and $INTL^*$ are mutually and simultaneously determined by a set of predetermined variables, X, whose behavior is assumed to be set outside of the system:

$$RD^* = \beta'_1 X + v_1 \tag{6.3}$$

$$INTL^* = \beta'_2 X + v_2 \tag{6.4}$$

RD^* and $INTL^*$, however, can only be observed as the dichotomous variables, RD and $INTL$. Hence, it is only possible to estimate β_1/σ_1 and β_2/σ_2, where $\sigma_1^2 = \text{Var}(v_1)$ and $\sigma_2^2 = \text{Var}(v_2)$, rather than β_1 and β_2 alone. Rewriting, with $RD^{**} = RD^*/\sigma_1$ and $INTL^{**} = INTL^*/\sigma_2$, the structural equations (6.1) and (6.2) are as follows:

$$RD^{**} = \gamma_1 \frac{\sigma_2}{\sigma_1} INTL^{**} + \frac{\beta'_1}{\sigma_1} X_1 + \frac{u_1}{\sigma_1} \tag{6.5}$$

$$INTL^{**} = \gamma_2 \frac{\sigma_1}{\sigma_2} RD^{**} + \frac{\beta'_2}{\sigma_2} X_2 + \frac{u_2}{\sigma_2} \tag{6.6}$$

To estimate these structural equations, we use the technique presented in Maddala.[12] We estimate the reduced forms (6.3) and (6.4) by the probit maximum likelihood method. These estimates are presented in tables 6–16 and 6–17. The predicted value, $\widehat{INTL}$ *(INTLHAT)*, is then substituted into the structural equation for R&D to yield the estimates in table 6–18. This corrects for the simultaneous equation bias inherent in the unadjusted, single-equation estimates in table 6–19. Similarly, the predicted value, $\widehat{RD}$ *(RDHAT)*, is substituted into the structural equation for *INTL* to yield the set of estimates in table 6–20. These can be compared to the unadjusted, single-equation estimates in table 6–21. The estimated coefficients in table 6–18 are $\gamma_1 \sigma_2/\sigma_1$ and β'_1/σ_1. The estimated coefficients in table 6–21 are $\gamma_2 \sigma_1/\sigma_2$ and β'_2/σ_2.

From table 6–18, we find that the effect of *INTL* on joint R&D, though still positive, is insignificant when the simultaneous determination of *INTL* and R&D is corrected for. We can see how the single-equation estimate compares with the simultaneous model estimate:

	Estimated Coefficient	t-Statistic
INTL	0.410	1.703
INTLHAT	0.877	0.957

From table 6–20, in contrast, we see that even when simultaneity is taken into account, R&D has a positive and significant exogenous effect

Table 6–16
Reduced Form Estimates of the Determinants of Joint R&D Activity, 1974–1982 Data

Independent Variable	Estimated Coefficient	Standard Error	t-Statistic
C (intercept)	− 2.872	0.456	− 6.296
POP	0.141E − 02	0.764E − 03	1.842
INDRD	0.148	0.587E − 01	2.516
FTECH	1.120	0.254	4.406
FPARTNER	0.680	0.252	2.698
GDPC	0.449E − 01	0.295E − 01	1.519
USRDS	− 2.865	4.698	− 0.610
MES	− 0.838E − 03	0.110E − 02	− 0.765
GOVT	0.323E − 01	0.248	0.130
MES-PCN	0.322	5.050	0.638E − 01
MEDIA	0.312E − 01	0.832E − 01	0.375
NONMEDIA	0.308E − 01	0.316E − 01	0.976
USSUB1	0.119	0.963	0.124
USSUB	− 0.399	0.967	− 0.413
EEC	0.351	0.255	1.374

Dependent variable: *RD*
Number of observations: 272
Mean of dependent variable: .15
Number of R&D joint ventures: 40
Number of non-R&D joint ventures: 232
$\chi^2(13) = 157.4$

Table 6–17
Reduced Form Estimates of the Determinants of Joint Venture Export Activity, 1974–1982 Data

Independent Variable	Estimated Coefficient	Standard Error	t-Statistic
C (intercept)	− 0.723	0.262	− 2.759
POP	− 0.379E − 03	0.724E − 03	− 0.524
INDRD	− 0.316E − 01	0.449E − 01	− 0.703
FTECH	0.785	0.231	3.398
FPARTNER	0.505	0.192	2.267
GDPC	− 0.165E − 01	0.235E − 01	− 0.703
USRDS	4.664	3.864	1.207
MES	0.720E − 03	0.719E − 03	1.001
GOVT	− 0.315	0.200	− 1.577
MES-PCN	5.752	3.898	1.476
MEDIA	− 0.900E − 01	0.598E − 01	− 1.506
NONMEDIA	0.385E − 01	0.240E − 01	1.601
USSUB1	1.710	0.676	2.531
USSUB	− 1.596	0.716	− 2.228
EEC	0.398	0.212	1.874

Dependent variable: *INTL*
Number of observations: 272
Mean of dependent variable: .37
Number of export joint ventures: 101
Number of nonexport joint ventures: 171
$\chi^2(13) = 308.6$

Table 6–18
Structural Estimates of the Determinants of Joint R&D Activity, 1974–1982 Data

Independent Variable	Estimated Coefficient	Standard Error	t-Statistic
C (intercept)	− 2.839	0.428	− 6.636
INTLHAT	0.877	0.916	0.957
POP	0.146E − 02	0.759E − 03	1.917
INDRD	0.162	0.517E − 01	3.133
FTECH	0.898	0.358	2.508
FPARTNER	0.518	0.312	1.660
GDPC	0.512E − 01	0.271E − 01	1.888
USRDS	− 3.621	4.500	− 0.805
MES	− 0.113E − 02	0.104E − 02	− 1.092
GOVT	0.479E − 01	0.258	0.182

Dependent variable: *RD*
Number of observations: 272
Mean of dependent variable: .15
Number of R&D joint ventures: 40
Number of non-R&D joint ventures: 232
$\chi^2(8) = 160.3$

Table 6–19
Unadjusted Single-Equation Probit Estimates of the Determinants of Joint R&D Activity, 1974–1982 Data

Independent Variable	Estimated Coefficient	Standard Error	t-Statistic
C (intercept)	− 2.720	0.347	− 7.835
POP	0.130E − 02	0.753E − 03	1.726
INTL	0.410	0.240	1.703
INDRD	0.164	0.519E − 01	3.167
FTECH	1.026	0.261	3.936
FPARTNER	0.599	0.251	2.388
GDPC	0.518E − 01	0.272E − 01	1.905
USRDS	− 3.233	4.484	− 0.721
MES	− 0.112E − 02	0.104E − 02	− 1.091
GOVT	0.297E − 03	0.240	0.124E − 02

Dependent variable: *RD*
Number of observations: 272
Mean of dependent variable: .15
Log of likelihood function: − 79.16
Number of R&D joint ventures: 40
Number of non R&D joint ventures: 232
$\chi^2(8) = 158.3$

Table 6–20
Structural Estimates of the Determinants of Joint Venture Export Activity, 1974–1982 Data

Independent Variable	Estimated Coefficient	Standard Error	t-Statistic
C (intercept)	− 0.583	0.235	− 2.480
RDHAT	1.663	0.586	2.839
MES-PCN	4.149	3.678	1.128
POP	− 0.906E − 03	0.728E − 03	− 1.245
MEDIA	− 0.659E − 01	0.550E − 01	− 1.199
NONMEDIA	0.149E − 01	0.228E − 01	0.653
USSUB1	1.413	0.634	2.229
USSUB	− 1.189	0.666	− 1.785
FPARTNER	0.106	0.198	0.536
EEC	0.230	0.205	1.120

Dependent variable: *INTL*

Number of observations: 272

Mean of dependent variable: .37

Number of export joint ventures: 101

Number of nonexport joint ventures: 171

$\chi^2(8) = 317.7$

Table 6–21
Unadjusted, Single-Equation Probit Estimates of the Determinants of Joint Venture Export Activity, 1974–1982 Data

Independent Variable	Estimated Coefficient	Standard Error	t-Statistic
C (intercept)	− 0.631	0.235	− 2.683
MES-PCN	4.584	3.614	1.268
POP	− 0.899E − 03	0.785E − 03	− 1.146
MEDIA	− 0.860E − 01	0.554E − 01	− 1.553
NONMEDIA	0.300E − 01	0.215E − 01	1.396
RD	0.621	0.241	2.574
USSUB1	1.419	0.636	2.231
USSUB	− 1.204	0.667	− 1.805
FPARTNER	0.286	0.176	1.619
EEC	0.371	0.193	1.925

Dependent variable: *INTL*

Number of observations: 272

Mean of dependent variable: .37

Number of export joint ventures: 101

Number of nonexport joint ventures: 171

$\chi^2(8) = 319.3$

on the joint venture's decision to export. The single-equation estimate is compared with the following simultaneous model estimate:

	Estimated Coefficient	t-Statistic
RD	0.621	2.574
RDHAT	1.663	2.839

Given, however that the estimated coefficient on *RDHAT* is really $\gamma_2 \sigma_2/\sigma_1$, we do not have a separate estimate, γ_2, to compare with the coefficient on *RD*.

This method provides a convenient first approximation to simultaneous equation models in the case of discrete, dependent variables. Additional precision can be obtained by correcting for possible bias in the standard error estimates and, hence, in the *t*-statistics reported here. The correction term is fairly complex.[13] Since the standard error is already quite low for the R&D estimates and quite high for the export estimates, the correction factor should not alter the results presented here.

Summary

Chapter 6 analyzes U.S.-foreign joint venture involvement in export operations. It identifies those factors that influence the decision of whether the joint venture will export to foreign markets or compete in the domestic market alone. It also considers the increasing percentage of joint ventures involved in export operations and suggests some possible reasons why joint ventures may be becoming more likely to seek export markets than in the past.

A probit maximum likelihood estimation technique is used to analyze a sample of 284 U.S.-foreign joint ventures formed between 1974 and 1982. Several factors appear to exert a positive influence on the likelihood of joint venture export activity: economies of scale in production, joint venture R&D, the foreign partner's presence in international markets, and the joint venture's location in the EEC. Other factors exert a negative influence: the market size of the host country and the media advertising intensity of the joint venture industry.

There is also evidence, however, that the relationship between the joint venture subsidiary and the operations of its U.S. parent firm affects joint venture export behavior. This makes the analysis somewhat different from an analysis of the export activity of an autonomous firm. The results indicate that highly international U.S. parent firms tend to form localized joint venture subsidiaries when the joint venture competes in the same primary SIC industry as the parent firm. When the joint venture produces dissimilar or peripheral product lines and, hence, poses less of a potential for conflict in third country markets, the joint venture is much more likely to export.

Notes

1. Paul R. Krugman, "Increasing Returns, Monopolistic Competition, and International Trade," *Journal of International Economics,* November 1979, pp. 469–479.

2. An interaction term between *MES-PCN* and *POP* was originally hypothesized but proved to be insignificant.

3. Oliver E. Williamson, *Markets and Hierarchies* (New York: The Free Press,1983), chapter 2.

4. R.E. Caves and J. Khalilzadeh-Shirazi, "International Trade and Industrial Organization: Some Statistical Evidence," in *Welfare Aspects of Industrial Markets,* A.P. Jacquemin and F.W. de Jong, eds. (Leiden: Martinus Nijhoff, 1977), pp. 114–115.

5. R.E. Caves, M.E. Porter, A.M. Spence, and J.T. Scott, *Competition in the Open Economy: A Model Applied to Canada* (Cambridge: Harvard University Press, 1980), p. 73.

6. Thomas Horst, "The Industrial Composition of US Exports and Subsidiary Sales to the Canadian Market," *American Economic Review,* March 1972, pp. 37–45.

7. Birgitta Swedenborg, *The Multinational Operations of Swedish Firms: An Analysis of Determinants and Effects* (Stockholm: Industrial Institute for Economic and Social Research, 1979).

8. Robert E. Lipsey and Merle Weiss, "Foreign Production and Exports in Manufacturing Industries," *Review of Economics and Statistics,* November 1981, pp. 488–494; and Swedenborg, *Multinational Operations,* pp. 116–118.

9. Two-tailed tests were used for variables with alternative sign predictions (*MEDIA, USSUB,* and *FPARTNER*). Otherwise, a one-tailed test was employed.

10. Information on the foreign partner's product line was not available. Hence, the effect of similar or dissimilar product lines was only testable for the U.S. firm.

11. Charles D. Mallar, "The Estimation of Simultaneous Probability Models," *Econometrica,* October 1977, pp. 1717–1721. For a clearer description of the method, see G.S. Maddala, *Limited-Dependent and Qualitative Variables in Econometrics* (Cambridge: Cambridge University Press, 1983), pp. 246–247.

12. See Maddala, *Limited-Dependent and Qualitative Variables in Econometrics,* p. 247.

13. Ibid.

7
Summary and Conclusions

This study has presented some new empirical findings on the recent characteristics of U.S.-foreign joint ventures in the manufacturing industries. It has further explored the determinants of two increasingly important characteristics of international joint venture activity: joint R&D and joint venture exports. The purpose of this final chapter is to provide an overview of the various issues covered by this research and to summarize the major empirical results.

There are some distinct differences between the characteristics of recent U.S.-foreign joint ventures and the types of international joint ventures formed prior to 1975. As a basis of comparison, this study has reviewed some of the earlier literature and data on international joint venture activity. By piecing together information from these various sources, this study has established a profile of traditional joint venture agreements between the early 1950s and 1975.

The analysis of traditional joint ventures covered several characteristics of international joint venture activity—the operations that international joint ventures were involved in, the location and geographical span of their activities, and the types of partners and ownership shares in the joint venture. Several interesting findings emerged. For example, in over two-thirds of the U.S.-foreign joint ventures formed between 1950 and 1975, manufacturing was the primary form of activity. In contrast, only about 15 percent of traditional U.S.-foreign joint ventures were primarily sales subsidiaries.

While traditional joint ventures may have typically been responsible for the manufacturing of their products, it appears that their span of control did not extend much further. There is little evidence, for example, of collaborative R&D operations, even as a secondary activity. Exports are another example. Information on these traditional joint ventures indicates that operations were, in most cases, restricted to production for the local market alone. It is interesting that the reasons for export restriction had less to do with joint venture profitability than with conflicts with the U.S. multinational parent's other, non-joint-venture operations. The joint venture's ability to expand into export markets was often effectively constrained by the U.S. parent's decision to serve these markets itself through other subsidiary operations.

Restrictions on exports, and most probably on R&D, hint at the type of parent–joint venture relationship that is central to our understanding of international joint venture activity. This book modeled three types of spillover effects between joint venture and parent firm profitability. In the first case, joint venture and non-joint-venture operations are completely independent. Consequently, the joint venture is free to pursue its own profit-maximizing behavior since its activities have no repercussions on the profits of the parent firm's other, non-joint-venture subsidiaries.

In the second case, spillovers are negative. The joint venture's activities may have a negative impact on the profits of the parent firm's non-joint-venture operations. We have seen evidence of this negative impact in traditional joint venture export activities. Joint venture exports, by competing with the sales of other, parent firm subsidiaries, resulted in a trade-off between joint venture and non-joint-venture profitability. Hence, joint venture exports were often restricted.

In the third case, positive spillovers may characterize the joint venture's relationship to other parts of its parent firm's operations. The parent firm, for example, may be able to apply know-how gained through the joint venture to other, non-joint-venture activities. The parent firm may also link the establishment of the joint venture to other profit-maximizing objectives. A recent example, described in chapter 3, involved the efforts of a U.S. multinational firm to regain access into a country that had been boycotting its products. In that particular case, Coca-Cola's partnership in an agricultural development joint venture in Egypt led to the subsequent lifting of the boycott on soft drink products. Whether or not the agricultural joint venture was profitable, the reinstatement of Coca-Cola's main line business into the lucrative Egyptian market was probably an important reason behind the joint venture agreement.

A major hypothesis of this book is, therefore, that the characteristics of international joint venture activity are influenced not only by the joint venture's profit-maximizing opportunities but also by the interdependence between a parent firm's joint venture and non-joint-venture profitability. With two parent firms, the joint venture is influenced by interdependence with two different parent firm networks. As the number of partners to the joint venture increases, the task of coordinating the joint venture's activities with the different goals and objectives of each of its parent firms becomes quite complex.

This model of joint venture and parent firm interaction was examined and tested in this study with recent data on U.S.-foreign international joint venture partnerships. In comparison to the characteristics of traditional joint venture activity, two findings are particularly significant.

The first is the larger percentage of joint ventures being formed to develop, manufacture, and market new product lines, as contrasted to the traditional joint venture strategy of producing and marketing the multinational partner's existing products. By 1982, about 20 percent of the new joint ventures in the sample were involved in collaborative R&D. The second particularly significant empirical finding involves the change in the percentage of international joint ventures exporting outside the host market. By the 1980s, about half of the new joint ventures formed each year exported to foreign markets. This trend contrasts with traditional joint ventures that tended to serve local markets alone.

Given the increasing importance of R&D and export operations in international joint venture activity, this study examines these findings further. It considers both the joint venture's profit-maximizing opportunities and the possibility of joint venture and parent firm interaction in seeking to understand some of the reasons affecting the decision to pursue collaborative R&D or to export from the joint venture subsidiary. The empirical results, based on qualitative choice econometric techniques, show that the joint venture's involvement in R&D or exports is, in fact, influenced by some of the same country-, industry-, and firm-specific factors that have been found to affect R&D or export activity among autonomous firms. In addition, however, the joint venture also appears to be affected by the interaction between its own activities and its parent firms' other, non-joint-venture operations as hypothesized.

Profits from R&D activities and, hence, the likelihood that the joint venture undertakes R&D as part of its operations were found to depend on several factors. These factors include the size of the local and international markets in which the joint venture intends to compete, market access, the technical competitiveness of the industry environment, and whether or not the joint venture has access to technical skills and resources.

Additional deterministic factors arising from the complex interrelationship between the joint venture's activities and the profits of other parent firm operations can affect the decision to undertake cooperative R&D. The minimum efficient scale of R&D operations, for example, was found to have a negative effect on the likelihood of joint venture R&D. If economies of scale in R&D are high, the parent firm may very well find it more profitable to centralize R&D in one location—most typically at the parent firm's home country in its own facilities. Hence, the likelihood of joint venture R&D may be reduced. There is also some evidence that the participation of an R&D-intensive U.S. parent in the joint venture may deter rather than encourage joint R&D efforts. This effect was most pronounced when the distribution of technical skills between parent firms was uneven. Since the R&D intensity of a parent firm may indicate the possession of proprietary technical know-how, it appears that U.S. firms may consider negative spillovers—in this case, the risks of sharing technical trade secrets—a deciding factor in whether or not to pursue collaborative R&D activities.

Both autonomous factors and an interdependence between parent firm and joint venture profitability also affected the likelihood of export activity. Overall, the model was fairly successful in identifying several of these factors. Factors that were positively identified with the joint venture's profit-maximizing motives for pursuing export markets included economies of scale in production, the joint venture's involvement in new product or process development, a foreign parent with operations in international markets, and joint venture location in the EEC. However, the larger the market size of the host country, the less likely that the joint venture would seek export markets. Similarly, a high media advertising intensity in the joint venture industry was negatively correlated with the likelihood of joint venture exports.

An issue that arose in the analysis of traditional joint venture activity was intersubsidiary competition in third country markets. This constraint on joint venture export activity was testable using the 1974–1982 database. The results showed a tendency for U.S. firms with highly international operations to form localized joint venture subsidiaries when the joint venture competes in the same primary SIC industry as the parent firm. When the joint venture produces dissimilar or peripheral product lines and, hence, poses less of a potential for conflict in third country markets, the joint venture is much more likely to export.

In conclusion, this book has provided some insight into a highly complex form of international business activity that has received surprisingly little attention in the business and economic literature. It has sought a better understanding of the types of partnerships being formed today and the factors affecting the choice of particular joint venture characteristics. Given the current popularity of U.S.-foreign partnerships in many industries, however, further research in this area seems to be in order. In particular, a more complete theory and empirical testing are needed to describe the coordination and control of a system of interconnected business units such as a firm's multinational network of subsidiary operations. The issue of joint venture activity then adds a further layer of complexity as it deals with the linkage between two or more sets of networks. Both partners must coordinate the joint venture's activities with other worldwide operations. For multinationals involved in several joint venture partnerships, this may involve coordinating agreements with one partner with the demands and objectives of other partners. This book has taken one step toward addressing some of the issues involved.

Appendix:
Variable Definitions

Variables Introduced in Chapter 5

R&D (RD): Dummy variable is set equal to 1 if the joint venture is involved in R&D operations and 0 otherwise.

Source: Own database. For each of the 420 joint ventures in the database, the information is screened for certain characteristics of the joint venture and its parent firms. One of these characteristics is the joint venture's intended pursuit of R&D activity. If the joint venture is mentioned as pursuing any type of new product or process development, the joint venture is characterized as involved in R&D activity. For more information on how this variable is compiled, see chapter 4.

Population (POP): The population of the foreign country in which the joint venture is based.

Source: Country data from the IMF's "International Financial Statistics." The mid-year estimates for the population of each country (line 99z) are used.

An alternative proxy for market demand that was initially considered was GDP data expressed in $U.S. at constant 1980 prices. The limitations of using existing exchange rates to convert the GDPs of different countries to a common currency, however, are problematic. A major difficulty is that exchange rates do not necessarily reflect the purchasing power of foreign currencies. Recent studies, most notably by Kravis et al.,[1] have sought a more accurate comparison of real product and purchasing power over different countries based on local expenditure data. For the purposes of this research, however, data on 56 countries for various years in a 9-year time period are required, which extends well beyond the scope of any available studies attempting to adjust GDP measurements for purchasing power across countries.

Industrial production indexes were also considered as a possible measure of market size. This would be especially appropriate where the joint venture produces and markets industrial products. Again, however, even though the IMF publishes industrial production figures for some countries in our sample (item 66c), the list is far from complete and suffers from similar difficulties of cross-country comparison.

International Exports (INTL): Dummy variable is set equal to 1 if the joint venture intends to market its products outside the host country and 0 if otherwise.

Source: Own database. For each of the 420 observations in the database, the data were screened for information pertaining to the geographic markets in which the joint venture was intending to compete. The level of detail in this database varied. Information on some joint ventures specified the countries to which the joint venture planned to export. Information on other joint ventures specified only that the joint venture planned to export some of its product. The data were, therefore, compiled at the most aggregate level, indicating whether or not there was mention of any export activity. For more information on how this variable was compiled, see chapter 4.

Industry R&D (INDRD): Average R&D expenditure as a percentage of net sales for all R&D companies in the joint venture's industry in the United States.

Source: National Science Foundation, *Research and Development in Industry, 1980*, table B–19, entitled *R&D funds as a percent of net sales in R&D-performing manufacturing companies by industry and size of company.* The data are based on an annual NSF survey of approximately 11,500 manufacturing and nonmanufacturing companies in the United States and grouped according to major SIC codes at either the two-digit or three-digit level of industrial classification. NSF data were available for 1974 to 1980.

A more disaggregate measure of industry R&D/Sales at the four-digit level is available from the Federal Trade Commission *Annual Line of Business Report.* As R&D intensity can vary within the broader two-digit and three-digit groupings, this alternative source of data was investigated. A large percentage of the joint venture data is classified at a 4-digit industry level, and hence, aggregating upward into broader SIC codes loses some of the information available.

Unfortunately, three problems existed with the FTC data. Foremost was the problem that for a large percentage of the four-digit industries, data were not available (this was the case for well over a third of the industries in any given year). Second, the data were only available for 3 (1974 to 1976) of the 9 years covered by this study. Finally, in the majority of the cases, three-digit and two-digit categories were not given to correspond to those joint ventures in our database that were classified at this broader level. A comparison of certain three-digit industries where both NSF and FTC R&D/Sales data existed showed some major discrepancies. In communications equipment (SIC no. 366), for example, the FTC estimates and R&D Sales ratio for the industry of 12.6 percent as compared to the NSF estimate of only 7.6 percent. Hence, the two databases were not compatible enough to combine in creating R&D/Sales estimates across industries.

The NSF data are therefore used to generate R&D/Sales estimates for the joint venture industries in our database. The major advantages over the FTC data are cross-industry completeness and longer time series availability. The limitations to keep in mind are the broader industry aggregations that lose some of the four-digit specificity of the joint venture data.

Foreign Technology (FTECH): Dummy variable is set equal to 1 if the foreign partner is judged to contribute technological know-how and resources to the joint venture and 0 if otherwise.

Source: Own database. The information in the database is screened for the instances in which the foreign firm is mentioned as contributing either product or process know-how to the joint venture. Examples of apparent contribution include cases where the foreign firm contributes products to the product line of the joint venture, cases where the foreign firm is mentioned as processing product or process technology beneficial to the joint venture, or cases where the foreign firm is responsible for process design or the contribution of unique high-technology production facilities. Examples of an apparent lack of contribution of product or process know-how include cases where the U.S. firm is mentioned as contributing the technology and the foreign firm the marketing skills, financing, or other nontechnical contributions. If no mention is made of the foreign firm's product or process know-how or contribution, it is assumed that the foreign partner is not making any important contributions to the joint venture in this way.

Omissions in the data provide a downward bias in our estimates of this variable across the sample. In some cases, for example, the foreign partner may contribute important product or process technology that is not mentioned in the published information on the joint venture. A second possible source of data on foreign technological capabilities was, therefore, considered to supplement this information. The Conference

Board published a 1982 report surveying the perceived technological capabilities of foreign firms in various industries.[2] One could, therefore, control for the joint ventures in our sample as being in one of the mentioned, technically advanced foreign countries, in an industry in which foreign competitors are perceived to be technically competitive with U.S. firms, and/or having a foreign partner that is specifically listed as being a technological leader in its industry.

A major problem with these data, however, was that the survey responses were not grouped according to any comparable industry classifications. Electronics, for example, was one industry in which foreign firms were perceived to be technologically superior to U.S. firms by many respondents. Other respondents, however, mentioned much more specific industry sectors such as solar cell array welding and communication-antennae technology. Noncompatibility across responses made these data particularly difficult for us to use. Hence, only the database presented in this research was used to estimate foreign technological capabilities.

Foreign Partner (FPARTNER): Dummy variable is set equal to 1 if the foreign partner operates in international markets outside its home country and to 0 if there is no indication of international scope in its operations.

Source: A listing of international subsidiaries of foreign corporations is available from any one of several publications (Dun & Bradstreet *Who Owns Whom* series and Moody's *International Manual*) depending on the nationality of the foreign firm.

In each case, the foreign partner or its corporate parent was identified and checked against this listing. If a distinct foreign partner was identified as separate from the joint venture entity and it operated one or more foreign subsidiaries, the variable *FPARTNER* was set equal to 1. No distinction, however, was made between foreign corporations that operated an entire network of foreign subsidiaries and those that had only one. As only 1983 data were available, there may be some error in the estimates as they apply to another year (that is, the year of joint venture formation). In some cases, a foreign partner that became international by 1983 was not so when the joint venture was formed. Fortunately, there do not appear to be many such cases. Foreign partners typically were either highly multinational entities with many foreign subsidiaries and affiliates, presumably not all of which were formed within the last few years, or small, local entities.

GDP per Capita (GDPC): The per capital GDP of the foreign country in which the joint venture is based. GDP data are expressed in $U.S. in constant 1980 prices. Population figures are based on annual IMF estimates for the year in which the joint venture is formed.

Source: Country data from the IMF's "International Financial Statistics." GDP figures in 1980 prices (line 99b.p) are translated to $U.S. by the end-of-year exchange rate (line ae) and divided by yearly population estimates (line 99z).

U.S. R&D/Sales (USRDS): R&D expense as a percentage of net sales for the U.S. parent firm.

Source: Total R&D expense/Net Sales for the U.S. firm can be obtained from either the Compustat or the Disclosure tapes on the PICA database. The Compustat data are available annually for the 9 years covered by our database (1974–1982). Disclosure data are only available for 1982 onward. Data, however, are only available at the most aggregate level of the U.S. firm's organization. If, for example, a U.S. subsidiary of a U.S. corporation formed a joint venture, R&D/Sales information is only available for the corporation as a whole.

In the majority of cases, the Compustat data were available to determine R&D/Sales for the U.S. parent firm in the year the joint venture was formed. For a few companies, Compustat data were not available for the year of joint venture formation. In that case, the next closest yearly estimates were taken. For a few other companies, no Compustat data on R&D/Sales were available. In those cases, Disclosure estimates were used. Finally, for about 20 percent of our sample, neither Compustat nor Disclosure data on R&D/Sales were available.

Minimum Efficient Scale (MES): The minimum efficient scale of R&D in the joint venture's industry.

Source: National Science Foundation, *Research and Development in Industry, 1980,* table B–22.

The 1980 report gives total company R&D expenditures of the first eight companies in each industry. It is thus possible to calculate the average R&D expenditure for this group of firms as an indication of the absolute minimum efficient scale of R&D in that industry. 1980 estimates are used for the whole time period in our sample since NSF data do not provide consistent industry groupings for this variable across different years. 1974 NSF data, for example, do not provide three-digit disaggregate figures for all the machinery manufacturing sector (SIC no. 35). 1980 NSF data, however, do. *MES* estimates can vary significantly between two-digit and three-digit classifications for a single industry and are, therefore, not comparable across time.

Government Involvement (GOVT): Dummy variable is set equal to 1 if the host country government actively promotes R&D activity by the foreign subsidiaries in its country and 0 otherwise.

Source: Behrman and Fischer list those countries that were found to offer specific inducements to foreign R&D activity.[3] Four countries were identified in which the pressure was most evident: Brazil, France, India, and Japan. The interviews on which these findings are based were conducted in spring and summer 1978, the midpoint of the database used in this research. Assuming that government policies did not change by very much in the 4 years prior and 4 years after 1978, we could use these countries as a rough proxy for the existence of government pressures to undertake local R&D.

Variables Introduced in Chapter 6

Minimim Efficient Scale in Production (MES-PCN): The minimum efficient scale of production activities in the joint venture's industry.

Source: 1977 Census of Manufactures Tape (U.S. Bureau of the Census). Available on the PICA database, variable C114. The Census Bureau has surveyed most manufacturing plants to determine the annual value of shipments for each plant. Each plant is then classified as belonging to one of eight different employment size classes, ranging from plants with 10 to 19 employees to those with over 2,500 employees. Information is available on the value of shipments for the size class containing median shipments for the industry, for the median and all higher classes, and for the whole four-digit SIC industry.

A measure of minimum efficient scale in production is derived by first summing up the shipments of plants in the median and all higher classes and then dividing this by the number of plants in these classes. This gives us the average annual value of shipments (in $U.S. million) at these size classes. This value is then divided by the value of the total industry shipments to yield a measure of relative minimum efficient scale comparable across industries. Where plants in the higher size classes ship, on average, a large percentage of total industry shipments, *MES-PCN* is defined as high for that industry. For industries where the average value of shipments is a smaller percentage of total industry shipments, *MES-PCN* is defined as being relatively low.

Two limitations on the data need to be kept in mind when using this variable. First, even though manufacturing plants may be defined as belonging to one four-digit SIC industry, a plant can make products belonging to several different industries. Similarly, for any given industry, plant data may be incomplete since plants classified as belonging primarily to other industries can also make products for this industry. Minimum efficient scale calculations may therefore, be distorted somewhat by this over- or undercounting of true output figures for a given industry. Since there is no satisfactory way of correcting for this problem, we assume here that the distortions are minor. In fact, given the large number of establishments surveyed (over 10,000 in some four-digit SIC industries), we can assume industry averages to be fairly accurate.

The second limitation has to do with missing observations in the data. For about 21 percent of the 420 observations in the database, data are not available from the Census Bureau survey to correspond to the industry in which the joint venture is classified. These gaps occurred for one of three reasons: (1) data were missing for a particular four-digit SIC industry, (2) the Census Bureau did not list the four-digit SIC industry in its coverage, or (3) the joint venture was classified at the three-digit or two-digit SIC level, aggregates on which the Census Bureau did not provide data. It was felt that the missing observations could be estimated by forming three-digit averages based on the available four-digit data. It is assumed that *MES-PCN* estimates are fairly similar within a given three-digit industry. Hence, these estimates were used to fill in the gaps in the data to achieve 100 percent coverage for this variable.

Media Expenditure/Sales (MEDIA): Ratio of media advertising expenditures to net sales for the joint venture industry.

Source: Federal Trade Commission, *Annual Line of Business Report.* Annual U.S. data at the four-digit SIC level available on the PICA database for 1974, 1975, and 1976, variable L483. This variable is the sum of traceable media advertising expense (PICA variable L408) and nontraceable media advertising expense (PICA variable L413) as a percentage of total sales and transfers in the industry (PICA variable L405). The average of the 1974, 1975, and 1976 data for each industry was used.

For about 15 percent of our sample, data on media expenditure were not available to correspond to the industry in which the joint venture was classified. This meant that neither four-digit SIC data were not available to correspond to a four-digit joint venture industry listing or that three-digit or two-digit SIC data were unavailable for the joint ventures classified into these more aggregate categories. Estimates were obtained for these missing observations by averaging over the available data in the four- or three-digit industry category.

Nonmedia Selling Expense/Sales (NONMEDIA): Ratio of nonmedia selling expenditure to net sales in the joint venture's industry.

NONMEDIA = SELLING – MEDIA. MEDIA has already been introduced above. *SELLING* (Selling Expense/Sales) is the ratio of total selling expenditure to net sales for the joint venture industry.

Source (for *SELLING*): Federal Trade Commission, *Annual Line of Business Report.* Annual data at the four-digit SIC level available on the PICA database for 1974, 1975, and 1976, variable L485.

SELLING captures more components of total marketing outlays than *MEDIA*, presumably including expenditures on sales force, media, and nonmedia promotions. On the PICA database, *SELLING* is generated as the sum of traceable media advertising expense (variable L408), other traceable selling expense (variable L409), nontraceable media advertising expense (variable L413), and other nontraceable selling expense (variable L414), divided by the total sales and transfers in the industry (variable L405).

Data on this variable are missing for 12 percent of the 420 observations in our sample. These gaps are estimated as they were for *MEDIA.*

U.S.-Foreign Subsidiary Sales/Net Sales (USSUB): Ratio of total foreign subsidiary sales to net sales for the U.S. parent firms of the joint ventures in our database.

Source: Compustat geographic segment data, available on the PICA database from 1977 onward, variable F1525. Where available, Compustat data on foreign subsidiary sales were matched with the U.S. parent firms of the joint ventures in our database. For the joint ventures formed between 1974 and 1976, 1977 geographic segment data were used as an approximation, being the earliest year available for this variable.

Unfortunately, despite the painstaking process of matching joint venture parent firms to Compustat data, data were missing for around 35 percent of the sample. Data could be missing for either of two reasons: (1) the joint venture parent was not a Compustat company—hence, no information was available on the firm; or (2) the joint venture parent was a Compustat company but no information was recorded on its foreign subsidiary sales. If the omission occurred for the second reason, the Compustat tapes were searched for the 3 years prior and 3 years after the joint venture was formed to see if the firm reported foreign subsidiary sales for any of those years. If it did, data for the nearest year were used as an approximation for the missing observations. This estimation technique reduced the number of missing observations somewhat to 32 percent of the sample. Since data for these neighboring years did, in most cases, indicate some degree of foreign subsidiary involvement, we could not say that missing data meant little or no foreign sales activity. Hence, we were not able to proxy missing data by 0s.

Other measures for the extent of the U.S. parent firm's international operations also suffered from substantial gaps in the available data. The ratio of export sales to net sales was generated where available. Even after estimating missing observations based on neighboring year data, however, more than 50 percent of the sample was unavailable. Furthermore, gaps in export data and foreign subsidiary data did not always occur for the same firms. Any aggregate measure of the U.S. firm's international involvement such as the ratio of export sales and foreign subsidiary sales to net sales would, therefore, be even more incomplete.

Joint Venture Located in EEC (EEC): Dummy variable is set equal to 1 if the joint venture is based in a country which is a member of the EEC and 0 if otherwise.

Source: The joint venture is located in the EEC if it is located in Belgium, Denmark, France, Germany, Ireland, Italy, Luxembourg, the Netherlands, the United Kingdom, or Greece (after 1981).

Notes

1. Irving B. Kravis, Alan Heston, Robert Summers. *World Product and Income: International Comparisons of Real Gross Product* (Baltimore: The Johns Hopkins University Press, 1982).

2. James R. Basche, Jr., "Technology Imports into the United States," *Research Bulletin*, 1983.

3. Jack N. Behrman and William A. Fischer, *Overseas R&D Activities of Transnational Companies* (Cambridge, Mass.: Oelgeschlager, Gunn & Hain, Publishers, Inc., 1980), pp. 108–110.

Bibliography

Amemiya, Takeshi. "Qualitative Response Models: A Survey." *Journal of Economic Literature*, December 1981, pp. 1483–1536.

Basche, James R., Jr. "Technology Imports into the United States." *Research Bulletin*, 1983.

Behrman, Jack N., and William A. Fischer. *Overseas R&D Activities of Transnational Companies.* Cambridge, Mass.: Oelgeschlager, Gunn & Hain, Publishers, Inc., 1980.

Bergsten, Fred C., Thomas Horst, and Theodore H. Moran. *American Multinationals and American Interests.* Washington, D.C.: Brookings Institution, 1978.

Brash, Donald T. *American Investment in Australian Industry.* Cambridge: Harvard University Press, 1966.

Caves, Richard E. *Multinational Enterprise and Economic Analysis.* Cambridge: Cambridge University Press, 1982.

Caves, R.E., and J. Khalilzadeh-Shirazi. "International Trade and Industrial Organization: Some Statistical Evidence." In *Welfare Aspects of Industrial Markets*, A.P. Jacquemin and F.W. de Jong, eds. Leiden: Martinus Nijhoff, 1977.

Caves, R.E., M.E. Porter, A.M. Spence, and J.T. Scott. *Competition in the Open Economy: A Model Applied to Canada.* Cambridge: Harvard University Press, 1980.

Curhan, J.P., W.H. Davidson, and R. Suri. *Tracing the Multinationals: A Sourcebook on U.S.-Based Enterprises.* Cambridge, Mass.: Ballinger Publishing Co., 1977.

de la Torre, Jose. "Exports of Manufactured Goods from Foreign Developing Countries: Marketing Factors and the Role of Foreign Enterprise." Ph.D. dissertation, Harvard Business School, Cambridge, 1970.

Flaherty, M. Therese. "Prices versus Quantities and Vertical Financial Integration." *Bell Journal of Economics*, Autumn 1981, pp. 507–525.

Franko, Lawrence G. *Joint Venture Survival in Multinational Corporations.* New York: Praeger Publishers, Inc., 1971.

Friedmann, W.G., and J.-P. Beguin. *Joint International Business Ventures in Developing Countries.* New York: Columbia University Press, 1971.

Friedmann, W.G., and George Kalmanoff, eds. *Joint International Business Ventures*. New York: Columbia University Press, 1961.

Goldberger, A.A. "Correlations between Binary Outcomes and Probabilistic Predictions." *Journal of the American Statistical Association*, March 1973, p. 84.

Grabowski, H.G., and N.D. Baxter. "Rivalry in Industrial Research and Development." *Journal of Industrial Economics*. vol. 22, 1973, pp. 209–235.

Horst, Thomas. "The Industrial Composition of U.S. Exports and Subsidiary Sales to the Canadian Market." *American Economic Review*, March 1972, pp. 37–45.

International Monetary Fund. *International Financial Statistics* (Yearbook), vol. 36, 1983.

Kamien, Morton I., and Nancy L. Schwartz. *Market Structure and Innovation*. Cambridge: Cambridge University Press, 1982.

Kravis, Irving B., Alan Heston, and Robert Summers. *World Product and Income: International Comparisons of Real Gross Product*. Baltimore, Md.: The Johns Hopkins University Press, 1982.

Mallar, Charles D. "The Estimation of Simultaneous Probability Models." *Econometrica*, October 1977, pp. 1717–1721.

Mansfield, E., A. Romeo, and S. Wagner. "Foreign Trade and U.S. Research and Development." *Review of Economics and Statistics*, February 1979, pp. 49–57.

Morrison, D.G. "Upper Bounds for Correlations between Binary Outcomes and Probabilistic Predictions." *Journal of the American Statistical Association*, March 1972, pp. 68–70.

Pindyck, Robert S., and Daniel L. Rubenfeld. *Econometric Models and Economic Forecasts*. New York: McGraw-Hill, 1976.

Porter, Michael E. *Competitive Strategy*. New York: The Free Press, 1980.

Raiffa, Howard. *The Art and Science of Negotiation*. Cambridge: Harvard University Press, 1982.

Scherer, F.M. *Industrial Market Structure and Economic Performance*. 2nd ed. Boston: Houghton Mifflin Company, 1980.

Schmookler, J. *Invention and Economic Growth*. Cambridge: Harvard University Press, 1966.

Stopford, John M., and Louis T. Wells, Jr. *Managing the Multinational Enterprise*. New York: Basic Books, Inc., 1972.

Swedenborg, Birgitta. *The Multinational Operations of Swedish Firms: An Analysis of Determinants and Effects*. Stockholm: Industrial Institute for Economic and Social Research, 1979.

Tomlinson, James W.C. *The Joint Venture Process in International Business*. Cambridge, Mass.: MIT Press, 1970.

Williamson, Oliver E. *Markets and Hierarchies: Analysis and Antitrust Implications*. New York: The Free Press, 1983.

Index

About the Author

Karen J. Hladik holds a Ph.D. in business economics from Harvard University and the Harvard Business School. She has studied in various countries abroad, including at Oxford University in England. In addition, she holds degrees in economics and chemical engineering from MIT, where she received Tau Beta Pi honors in engineering and Sigma Xi honors in research. Her areas of specialty are international economics and business policy, and she has taught and consulted on various topics in these areas.

Dr. Hladik is currently an economist in the Corporate Planning Department at Exxon Corporation in New York. She enjoys foreign languages and countries and has traveled extensively throughout the world.